LOVE
LETTER
FROM
PIG

LOVE

My Brother's Story of Freedom Summer

LETTER

Julie Kabat

FROM

University Press of Mississippi / Jackson

PIG

The University Press of Mississippi is the scholarly publishing agency of
the Mississippi Institutions of Higher Learning: Alcorn State University,
Delta State University, Jackson State University, Mississippi State University,
Mississippi University for Women, Mississippi Valley State University,
University of Mississippi, and University of Southern Mississippi.

www.upress.state.ms.us

The University Press of Mississippi is a member
of the Association of University Presses.

This work depicts actual events as truthfully
as recollection permits and/or can be verified by research.

First printing 2023
∞

Library of Congress Cataloging-in-Publication Data

Names: Kabat, Julie, author.
Title: Love letter from Pig : my brother's story of Freedom Summer / Julie Kabat.
Other titles: My brother's story of Freedom Summer
Description: Jackson : University Press of Mississippi, [2023] | Includes
bibliographical references and index.
Identifiers: LCCN 2023017542 (print) | LCCN 2023017543 (ebook) | ISBN
9781496847232 (hardcover) | ISBN 9781496847249 (epub) | ISBN
9781496847256 (epub) | ISBN 9781496847263 (pdf) | ISBN 9781496847270 (pdf)
Subjects: LCSH: Kabat, Luke. | Mississippi Freedom Project—Biography. |
African Americans—Suffrage—Mississippi—History—20th century. | Civil
rights workers—Mississippi—History—20th century. | Civil rights
movements—Mississippi—History—20th century. | African
Americans—Mississippi. | Mississippi—Race relations—History—20th century.
Classification: LCC E185.98.K33 A6 2023 (print) | LCC E185.98.K33 (ebook)
| DDC 323.1196/07307620904—dc23/eng/20230503
LC record available at https://lccn.loc.gov/2023017542
LC ebook record available at https://lccn.loc.gov/2023017543

British Library Cataloging-in-Publication Data available

Dedicated to my grandchildren
Sam, Sarah, Ben, Luca, and Bianca

I am fighting a nonviolent battle because I believe
that hate begets hate and perhaps that love begets love.

—LUKE KABAT, unpublished diary

CONTENTS

Part Four: Outcomes and Carrying On

LETTER AND PREFACE

Dear Luke,

Here is your story. I hope I have done it justice.

Glancing at a handwritten outline for the book you intended to write, I am saddened that you never had the chance to fulfill this dream. So it is, along with your other dreams for a flourishing life. You died too soon—a mere two years after Freedom Summer. I look back now over many, many years, understanding that your story is still vital in our world. It connects us to untold others because it is a quintessential story of America—the struggle for what we stand for, for what America means. The book is a combination of biography and memoir.

I am very grateful that you enjoyed writing so that I, and others, may climb inside your story, much of it in your own words. Your friends and coworkers have also been generous in sharing their recollections and writings. Our mother wanted to write a book, and she even sketched parts of a play, to honor you. This is a gift for her too.

Love,

Pig

Freedom Summer

In 1964, the apartheid state of Mississippi wavered on the brink of a historic reckoning. For as long as could be remembered, African Americans had endured violent resistance against any attempt they made to achieve equal rights and justice. Desperate to succeed in their quest, civil rights leaders took an unusual step. They decided to recruit a large number of northern volunteers for the Mississippi Summer Project (later renamed Freedom Summer).

My brother Luke was one of over a thousand mostly white northern volunteers who spread across the state that summer. They joined a grassroots movement already well underway and pledged to adhere to the philosophy of nonviolence, which was central to the mission. The northern volunteers were able to lend support to the thousands of local African American activists and community members of all ages who challenged the myths of white supremacy and began to break down the power of the Ku Klux Klan.

At the heart of Mississippi Freedom Summer was the voter-registration drive. To attain the equality and freedom they sought, Blacks needed to gain political power. Out of the African Americans in Mississippi, only a tiny fraction (6.4 percent) was registered to vote. But whites in Mississippi who ran the county election boards believed fervently that registering Blacks would deliver a mortal blow to their way of life. Whites did whatever they could to resist it. If you were Black, just *trying* to register to vote could entail losing your job, being beaten, tortured, or even murdered.

To mitigate the risks, instead of asking Blacks to try to register through normal channels, civil rights leaders decided to form a new and integrated political party—the Mississippi *Freedom* Democratic Party. They followed all the steps necessary to make sure that this new political party was legal. To show that Blacks really *did* want to vote, despite denials to the contrary by whites, it would be necessary to register as many people as possible. "One Man, One Vote" was the rallying cry.

Community centers throughout the state were meant to serve not only as headquarters for the voter-registration drive but also as hubs for education. They contained libraries stocked with donated books. They provided adults with job training and education in literacy and public health plus workshops on home improvement and other topics of interest. They were open to young children, teaching reading and offering opportunities for recreation.

Freedom Schools, intended for teenagers, also played an essential role. While voter registration was the immediate goal, Freedom Schools were conceived as catalysts for long-term change. Classes were to focus on relevant subjects, such as citizenship and Black history. Teaching methods would introduce students to critical thinking. The plan was for students' summer studies to culminate in a student-led Freedom School convention, bringing student representatives from all around the state to debate practical youth policies aimed at bettering society. A "Prospectus for the Summer," which was sent in early spring to prospective volunteers, predicted: "By the end of the summer, the basis will have been laid for a cadre of student leadership around the State of Mississippi committed to critical thinking and social action."

The organizers who planned the Mississippi Summer Project understood that young African Americans constituted their most natural constituency and were a great, untapped resource. Freedom Schools would reach these youths. On the flip side, they thought that parents, who might be reluctant to support the civil rights movement, could be tempted to follow the example of their children and be drawn in or at least not resist it.

Freedom Summer was a bold experiment in creating social change from the ground up. As Gail Falk, Luke's fellow volunteer, wrote in retrospect, "Violence against civil rights activists continued sporadically into the latter part of the 1960s, but the black citizens of the state had learned they didn't have to react to intimidation with fear and paralysis."

On Language

Living languages breathe and change, responding to shifts in perception and customs. These changes, like footprints, allow us to trace the historical journey we've taken. Beginning in 1619, in the New World of the American colonies, there was *slavery* and there were *slaves* who were kidnapped from Africa—a horrific injustice based on the rationale of white supremacy. Today, we are learning to refer to the exploited and vulnerable people who built our country not as *slaves* but as *human beings* and the *enslaved*, so that the action foisted upon these people is captured in the language. The language used is no longer a noun, a *thing*, but an *act* of subjugation committed by the enslaver. Over time, there were *freedmen* and *freedwomen*, the relatively lucky ones, in addition to slaves. For over two centuries, masters and mistresses—the owners of human property—adopted the widely used term *colored* and a long list of other terms as well. In 1920, the US Census incorporated the term *negro*. During the following decade, the scholar and civil rights activist W. E. B. Du Bois led a campaign urging publications to capitalize the word. In one of his letters, Du Bois wrote that he saw "the use of a small letter for the name of twelve million Americans and two hundred million human beings as a personal insult." In 1930, the *New York Times* stated that their reporters would now capitalize the word *Negro* and that this was "not merely a typographical change . . . but recognition of racial self-respect for those who have been for generations in the 'lower case.'"

In 1964, *Negro* was the commonly accepted written form of the word. In this book, I quote from many different primary sources, including Luke's letters and diaries, those written by his friends, and contemporary news reports. Within quotes—in the language of the time, the word *Negro* appears often.

Not long after Mississippi Freedom Summer, *black* (usually written with a lower case *b*) came into wider use as it was associated with the emerging concepts of *Black Power* and *Black is beautiful*. As the civil rights movement continued into the latter 1960s, the word *black* replaced *Negro*. After all, slave owners had coined the term *Negro* long ago, so the word implies white supremacy. Why should enslavers continue to own the language?

In the 1960s, many people also began to use the term *Afro-American*. This was standardized in the 1980s into *African*

American. Black is a global term, a color, that refers to a person anywhere in the world who belongs to the African diaspora. *African American* links someone not only to one's heritage but also to the landscape and geography of home. Referring to both ancestry and land, the term parallels other ethnicities, such as *Asian American, Italian American,* and *Native American.*

Today, with a spotlight on issues of racism in the national press, most publications are capitalizing *Black* to show respect. Many writers toggle back and forth between *Black* and *African American.* There is also a new discussion, very much in flux, about whether to capitalize the word *white* for someone of European descent. Since I am writing about a historical period during which the question did not arise—and it is not a matter of being respectful—I use lower case *white.*

Language evolves and, hopefully, so does our understanding not only of the world we live in but also the world that came before.

Any discriminatory or derogatory language or hate speech regarding race, ethnicity, religion, sex, gender, class, national origin, age, or disability that has been retained in this book is in no way an endorsement of the use of such language outside a scholarly context and appears only in direct quotes made at the time.

Part One

PREPARATION

① I'm in a restaurant without paper & feel
like writing so I shall use napkins & hope
that you can read what I write

Dear Family —

I'm thru finals & did well on
all of them — including Genetics ~~at it~~
~~Total of smit~~ — Tomorrow I'll
spend the day with Alix and then
it will be 2 weeks of preparation
for boards — I feel well prepared
after 3 years of hard grinding and
dont anticipate much problem with
the ~~Boards exam~~ exams. I am
going to go to Mississippi — You
want reasons why so I'll give you
a few. I wrote in my application
for SNCC that I wanted Negroes
to have equal opportunities — This
is the obvious reason that anybody
works for civil rights — Because the
Negroes have been cruelly deprived of
their rights. The State of Miss has
neglected its responsibility to its Negro
citizens and therefore it is necessary for
"outsiders" to remind them that the
rest of the Nation is concerned and won't
stand for any more ~~subjugation of the Negroes~~

Chapter 1

A TEST OF FAMILY VALUES

Luke's letter scribbled on a napkin was postmarked June 1, 1964. Our parents had been forewarned about his plans, but it didn't seem to matter. My oldest brother, Luke, had told them when he was applying to volunteer for the Mississippi Summer Project, but they went nuts anyway. They were flooded by fear. He wrote:

> I recognize the possibility of danger in Mississippi, but I really have confidence that no physical harm will be done to me. I have talked with many individuals in the Civil Rights Movement—Negroes and whites who are working in Mississippi. They are alive and healthy and so I shall be healthy too.
>
> I don't want to sit back while Negroes are being denied their rights—
>
> I don't want to "let others do it" because it is <u>my</u> responsibility <u>too</u>.

Flustered, they phoned him immediately. Dad stood alone upstairs, nervously clutching the phone to his one good ear. From the windows of his small study, he gazed out at dancing waves on the Narragansett Bay, perhaps hoping that the familiar motion would soothe him. Mom listened in on the phone downstairs, heaving heavy sighs. As was often the case, I pretended to be invisible, keeping all my senses on high alert.

"We need to talk about it," Dad insisted. "You've got to come home, Luke." His voice was soft but urgent.

In hopes of dissuading him, they demanded that Luke fly across the country from California back to Rhode Island.

But, in his letter, Luke had already staked his ground. "I would like you to just wish me luck and realize that I am doing a good and necessary job—that you brought up a son who is sort of a nutty idealist but not really so nutty."

I knew deep in my bones that Luke and all of us children were raised to be idealistic. It was woven into the lore and the very DNA of our family. *What's wrong now?* I wondered. *Why are they so afraid?*

✦ ✦ ✦

As soon as Luke agreed to come home, our parents concocted a plan. Convinced they couldn't succeed on their own, they enlisted me. Mom proposed a deal while Dad stood behind her, nodding. Luke and I could stay nights by ourselves in the log cabin. Our big house sat atop a steep hill that sloped in three levels down to a rocky beach. Built originally as a small guesthouse, the cabin nestled among bushes on the first level below the house. It served as an outpost for family visits and summer sleepovers. During the day and for meals, we'd come up to the house. Their condition was that when Luke and I were alone I must persuade him *not* to go. It was also imperative, Mom explained, that I was not to reveal that I was doing this at their bidding. I was annoyed they were asking me to be their *secret* emissary. *Why do they keep doing this to me?* I thought, but I deeply missed my brother. Despite the subterfuge, I agreed.

Secrets functioned as a currency in our family, especially for Mom. Listening now to her pleading, a childhood memory floated back to mind. At the time, my sister, Alix, was about nine and I, about four.

The day Alix brought home a new puppy, she towered over me. "You can't pet Jazzy 'cuz he's mine!"

As usual, Mom backed her up, hoping to avoid a tantrum. *Be nice to Alix* was a watchword repeated by both my parents.

The secret Mom and I shared was that when Alix was out of the house, I could pet Jazzy to my heart's content but only on the condition that I kept a safe distance while she was home. Luckily, Alix softened over time, and Jazzy became the family dog. This was one ruse among many. When Mom sensed there was something I wanted, she might offer a bargain. A secret was often part of the price.

Now seventeen, I had just graduated a year early from high school. Being the youngest of four, I was the only child still living at home. To me, the house felt big and rambling with just my parents and my grandmother Bubbe for company. Like most teenagers, I didn't consider hanging out with the old folks the best way to spend my time. I especially missed my oldest brother, Luke.

Like Luke, my brother David and sister, Alix, were living far away. They, too, were studying in California—David at the California Institute of Technology (Caltech) for graduate school and Alix at college in Berkeley. Perhaps it wasn't surprising that all three of my siblings had drifted out west since our family had lived there when they were in their teens. David was mischievous, fond of teasing me, and he had a piercing sense of humor. Sometimes when he was a teenager, he hid behind the trees outside our home, tossing mud pies when I unsuspectingly walked out of the house and down the steps. His aim was flawless. My sister, Alix, liked being alone in her own fantasy world or outdoors observing nature. She spent hours reading and drawing or watching birds and gathering plants for study. To her, I was a younger pest. She didn't welcome my overtures, so we lived almost separate lives.

Although Luke was now a student at Stanford Medical School, he had lived at home for three years when he was in college. We had always been close, but during that time, I became his good buddy, no matter that eight long years separated us. His bedroom was in a separate wing off to the side of the house in what once might have been maid's quarters. From my upstairs bedroom window, I could look down over the roof of his room. At all hours, I heard strains of classical music that he played on his stereo to help him study. The house was drafty, built as a summer home without insulation, each room with a lonely hissing radiator, but whatever the season, it always felt cozy when Luke was home.

In those years, Luke and I often hung out together in the cluttered kitchen surrounded by Mom's antiques. The open shelves were stuffed with her mismatched dishes, and the counters and walls were deep yellow and blue. Whenever he was preparing for exams, Luke would ask me to choose questions at random from a list he provided, and in this way, I learned about the history, literature, or language he was studying. For instance, the question of why President Lincoln issued the Emancipation Proclamation was scrawled on one list while, on another, words to be translated into Spanish fairly jumped off the page. We two talked for hours on end. No subject was off limits in our wide-ranging conversations.

Now I was thrilled I'd be seeing my oldest brother again. He was preparing to take the medical board exams in about two weeks and would be home as soon as he could manage after that. I also realized, however, that there was a hitch to the agreement I'd made with my parents. Luke expected me to be honest. He'd said so at the end of his letter: "Please write me a letter Pig. Tell me how you feel about my summer plans as I have the greatest respect for your opinions."

Pig... I thought it was endearing he still used my old nickname.

As a toddler, I was told, I had pulled myself up by the bars along the edge of my crib and declared, "Pig [meaning 'Big Julie'] stood!" It had been a tease at first when my brothers mimicked how I mispronounced the word *big*, but the nickname stuck.

✦ ✦ ✦

When Luke arrived, he paused in the doorway of the kitchen where my mother, grandmother, and I were waiting.

The three of us grinned, our arms outstretched for hugs, exclaiming in a jumble, "He's here! Oh look! He's here!"

And there stood my brother with his slight frame, dark chiseled features in a long face, and silver specks in his prematurely graying hair. Dad followed close behind carrying Luke's suitcase, barely noticed in the commotion.

That same evening, Luke and I moved into the log cabin. Quaint and furnished with antiques that Mom collected, there was a living room, a small kitchen at the back, two bedrooms, and an unscreened front porch. The cabin perched on rocks overlooking the bay. Through the open windows, you could hear the gentle surf.

Whenever my parents caught me up at the house without Luke around, they whispered, "Have you talked to him? Did you tell him not to go?" Pretending to be dutiful, I'd nod with lips pursed but remain silent. They never seemed to notice my squinting eyes that telegraphed my honest answer. I felt trapped because I didn't want to lie. However, I couldn't find a way to utter a single word to discourage my brother. Why would I? I was young, totally basking in his courageous aura, and certain I could never change his mind. When he said he'd be safe, I believed him.

Luke, at twenty-five, had just finished his third year at Stanford. By studying to be a doctor, he was following in Dad's footsteps. Our father, Herman, was beloved by his patients for his soft-spoken manner and his groundbreaking work in physical rehabilitation. Luke had just passed his finals and board exams, which meant he was free from academic pressure for the first time in years. The summer beckoned. Why wouldn't he go? He appeared to harbor no doubts.

When we were alone in the cabin, Luke told me about Mahatma Gandhi: how Gandhi had developed the practice of *satyagraha*, nonviolent civil resistance, to oppose British rule in India. For years growing up, we had listened whenever our mother told us compelling family stories about her father and her brother fighting oppression and tyranny in Russia and in Spain. Mom was a voracious reader who never gave up studying literature and theater. Always the romantic, she laced her stories with flowery language and dramatic flourishes. In the stories, her father and brother played starring roles.

Her father, called Ber-Leib in the Old Country, had joined the ill-fated 1905 revolution, hoping to overthrow the czar's cruel regime. He was imprisoned, and his brother, an orator known as Golden Voice, helped him escape and flee out of Russia by night, hidden under straw in a horse-drawn cart. Luke and I knew our grandfather only through Mom's stories. We never had the chance to meet him because he died long before we were born. Now in the cabin hearing Luke talk about Gandhi and the principle of nonviolence, it occurred to me for the first time to wonder whether our grandfather had ever carried a gun.

We did know Mom's oldest brother, our Uncle Sam, who visited us every couple of years. In the late 1930s, about two years before Luke was born, Sam had fought in the Spanish Civil War. A labor organizer, he had joined the Lincoln Brigade, which was the first American military force to include whites and Blacks on equal terms. Like all volunteers who served in the International Brigades, Uncle Sam hoped to save democracy by defeating fascism. General Francisco Franco led the monarchists, who found allies in Adolf Hitler and Benito Mussolini. During the Spanish civil war, Hitler tried out military strategies he later employed to great effect in World War II. Unfortunately, the other democracies of Europe paid lip service to the importance of saving democracy in Spain but did not provide military aid or troops. Sam fought on the losing side.

Luke admired Uncle Sam. When he visited, they usually had long conversations. I liked to listen, but the last time they had caught me off guard.

Sam admitted he was disillusioned and rethinking his politics.

Hearing this, Luke was furious and barked, "No! What about your ideals? You can't turn your back on your own good deeds!"

"Oh Luke," Sam shot back, "hear me out now."

Early in his service, Sam had been wounded. When he was taken behind the front lines for medical treatment, he saw Russian officers dressed in fancy uniforms, drinking wine, and eating meat.

"They were living like kings. That's not what communism promised," Sam declaimed. "On the front lines we were practically starving. These officers were calling the shots from a safety zone while we were facing imminent danger. It wasn't right!"

Luke was not swayed.

I had to admire my brother's persistence. Luke's hot temper frightened me, but nonetheless, I was his biggest fan. No one else came close to having such strong convictions. I loved my brother's passionate desire to stay true to his ideals.

✦ ✦ ✦

In the cabin, Luke explained how Gandhi had introduced a whole new way of "fighting" by holding to the moral high ground of nonviolence. In Mom's telling of the family tales, I realized, she'd romanticized everything and skirted around the issue of violence. Instead, she highlighted the idea of fighting for a just cause. In Mississippi, Luke said he'd need to pledge to practice Gandhi's principles. Doing so would take a great deal of self-control, discipline, and courage.

Always the passionate teacher, Luke taught me other things too. For instance, he sketched diagrams to explain how the menstrual cycle works to help me understand what was going on in my changing body. My parents were so shy about talking about the birds and the bees that they'd barely said a word.

They'd asked me just one question about babies. "Do you know?"

They seemed so relieved when I muttered, "yes," they never broached the subject again.

Unlike our parents, Luke wasn't shy and was used to thinking in straightforward scientific terms.

These conversations brought back the feeling of old times when I was eleven to fourteen and Luke was living at home, commuting to the University of Rhode Island. We would often hang out, talking at the round kitchen table. Our grandmother Bubbe worked around us, quietly listening, as the kitchen filled with the penetrating scents of stews and sauces she laced with copious quantities of onions.

During these years, David and Alix were focused on their own lives and were not as present at home. David was only sixteen months younger than Luke, and they'd always been close. As teenagers in California, they had challenged each other to endless rounds of basketball in the backyard, and they talked about everything they encountered on a daily basis. But by this time, David was off at college, living on campus at Brown University in Providence. He came home briefly for holidays and weekends but only once in a while. Alix was three years younger than David and busy at first in her last years of high school and then went off to college far away at the University of California in Berkeley. Almost five years younger than Alix, I trailed behind my siblings, like a caboose on a long train.

Although Luke was eight years older, he treated me like an equal, and I never questioned the bond we had. He took me along on social occasions with his friends. He enjoyed bringing me to the university's science lab after hours to repeat a class experiment that he'd done earlier in the day. As a premed student, he was majoring in zoology.

I still remember . . .

"Hey Pig, let's go," Luke would say. He'd turn and walk away, nonchalantly waving for me to follow him.

Like an eager puppy, I always did. Usually, we climbed onto the front seat of the family station wagon, a 1956 Pontiac, slammed the

Luke at home in Plum Beach, Rhode Island. Courtesy of the author.

big doors shut and rolled down the windows. Slipping the key into the ignition, Luke would hesitate. Had he forgotten something?

His fingers fumbled for his breast pocket. He smiled as he pulled out a battered harmonica. "OK, Pig, name this tune."

A raucous folk melody floated in the air. He played it again and again until I identified it correctly. Then, with his wobbly voice supporting mine, we sang the whole song. Like this one:

In Dublin's fair city, where the girls are so pretty
'Twas there that I first met sweet Molly Malone
She wheeled her wheelbarrow thru streets broad and narrow
Crying, "cockles and mussels alive alive-o!"

She was a fishmonger but sure 'twas no wonder
For so were her father and mother before

*And they each wheeled their barrow thru streets broad
    and narrow
Crying, "cockles and mussels alive alive-o!"*

*She died of a fever, and no one could save her
And that was the end of sweet Molly Malone
Her ghost wheels her barrow thru streets broad and narrow
Crying, "cockles and mussels alive alive-o!"*

Ready then, he fired up the car, and we'd be off. Bouncing down the road with no seat belts, windows rolled all the way down and the breeze whipping our hair, we'd laugh and talk as we sped up and down hills through the woods to the University of Rhode Island.

✦ ✦ ✦

But now up at the house, there was no time to reminisce. Our parents fretted and schemed. They confronted Luke and wheedled as best they could. Mostly, I recall Dad, as he usually did in contentious situations, hovering behind Mom and quietly egging her on.

"Tell him." He leaned closer. "Go on . . . tell him."

After a pause, Mom began cajoling, "But Lucien dear, you have so many other, more important things you can do when you're a doctor."

I noticed she'd used his real name to make her point.

Pulling her shoulders back and standing tall, she reminded him, "You don't *need* to do this."

Luke was steadfast.

"Don't you understand?" she scolded, scrunching up her face. "Lucien, listen to us." Her voice slid an octave higher. "They don't need *you!*" Her eyes flashed and she hissed, "It's crazy for you to go!"

Luke glared at them. "It's so easy for you to spout the words with all your highfalutin' principles and grand ideas, but I want to see you *act* on them!" He spread his arms wide. "And you can." Pointing, as if driving a stake into the ground, he bellowed, "Right *here!*"

Luke frowned and closed his eyes, seeing the world that he'd shared with them crumbling. He paused for a moment, then opened his eyes, gritted his teeth, and muttered, "I can't believe this."

Throughout their arguing, I wanted to disappear. I held my body stiffly still, my eyes most likely wide open and fearful.

Luke was pained to realize that Mom and Dad didn't accept his point of view. After all, they'd raised him to believe in the principles of equality and the need to stand up for one's beliefs, but now, perhaps, they were showing their true colors. I knew that in the past, unlike now, they'd encouraged him to be adventurous. In college, he'd hitchhiked alone across the country far into Mexico two summers in a row. They hadn't seemed overly worried then. What's more, he had the example that Dad set when he had stood up for his principles and lost his job in the mid-1950s during Joseph McCarthy's anticommunist witch hunt: the reason we'd moved away from California to Rhode Island. I didn't think their arguments added up, and besides, in every family fight, I inevitably took Luke's side.

Why aren't they congratulating him for his courage? I wondered. *Why's Mom begging him not to go? Don't they trust him?* Behind the scenes, out of my sight, there was more going on than I knew, but at the time, I had no clue.

Then, on June 22, ten days before he was to depart, a shocking announcement broke on the TV evening news. Three young men had gone missing in Mississippi, two white volunteers from the North—Mickey Schwerner and Andrew Goodman—and a local African American, James Chaney. The story dominated the news. We all crowded into Bubbe's small bedroom off the kitchen and stared at the TV, unable to move: Bubbe in her rocking chair; Luke, Mom, and I sitting on the edge of our chairs; Dad standing nearby, wringing his hands together and biting his lips. The circumstances as they emerged were horrifying.

The next day, President Lyndon Johnson ordered J. Edgar Hoover to send in an FBI team to investigate. At long last after years of neglect, the federal government and the news media were paying attention to the dire situation and the violence perpetrated against Blacks in Mississippi. Mom especially, barely breathing, stayed glued to the TV. Reporters announced that the FBI had found the station wagon the three young men had been driving. It was burned and still smoldering. But the bodies of the men were not in the car. Journalists said they had *disappeared*. Had they been murdered?

Mickey's wife, Rita, was convinced they were dead, but no one could say for sure. She demanded that President Johnson increase the FBI's involvement in the search.

When the president tried to console her, she rebuked him by reminding him, "This is not a social call."

When interviewed by the media, she declared fiercely, "It is tragic, as far as I am concerned, that white Northerners have to be caught up in the machinery of injustice and indifference in the South before the American people register concern."

I glanced at Luke sitting beside me and saw tears welling up in his eyes. And yes, tragically, we knew that Rita Schwerner was right. Without the death of the white boys, no one in the media would be paying attention. Neither would we. This was not a comforting insight.

Paul Johnson, the governor of Mississippi, declared it was all a publicity hoax engineered by the young men themselves who must be in Cuba by now. From his point of view, like many other white people in the South, anyone who opposed segregation had to be an atheist and thus a communist. James Silver, a liberal history professor at the University of Mississippi, was interviewed on TV. Earlier, he had written a controversial exposé called *Mississippi: The Closed Society* (1964).

Professor Silver issued a warning. "No one else should come down here. If you do, you'll be killed" was his message.

Mom let out a bloodcurdling scream that ripped right through me. Her worst fears were justified. And now, for the first time, I understood her. I felt terrified but said nothing. I was caught between conflicting emotions.

I thought, *Oh Luke, they're right! I see it now. Don't go!* But I immediately countered this with a question: *How can you back down now just when you're really needed there?* I felt my eyes crossing with confusion. I had to admit I didn't know what he should do. I looked at him in search of an answer.

Luke was peering straight ahead into the distance as if looking at a future that the rest of us couldn't see. He was unwavering in his commitment. Loyalty to my brother won out.

His fights with Mom and Dad soon escalated. Luke was finding it hard to control his fiery temper.

He often grew red in the face, shouting, "Of course, I'm going. Leave me alone!" He stomped out of the kitchen and slammed the door behind him.

In the past, Luke and Mom had their share of heated arguments. Throughout his high school and college years, she was always pleading with him to cut his hair.

"It's too long!" she'd whine.

"Just leave me alone!" he'd yell. "What's the big deal?"

He'd never listened or obeyed her then, no matter how angry she got. The stakes were higher now, but the outcome was the same.

Dinners became tense. Little by little, less was said out loud. In conversation, Mom, Dad, and Luke began dancing more politely around each other. I held my breath and watched. I was glad things were calmer even if much was left unsaid.

Down in the cabin, Luke and I still had fun snatches of conversation. We took a long walk together on the beach, leaping over rocks and basking in the sun. We swam in the bay. I relished the time I had alone with him.

Soon, Luke would be flying on a plane to Memphis for an orientation that would prepare him for the summer's work ahead.

Luke had told me the volunteers would need to learn how to practice nonviolent resistance. For instance: What do you do when someone spits in your face? When you're arrested, or beaten? How do you fall to the ground and go limp instead of following your instinctive impulse to fight back?

I wondered how Luke would do learning all this. I realized I would find it hard to do, and my temper was mild compared to his. Thinking about his arguments with Mom, I worried, *Maybe he won't be able to stay calm in Mississippi. What if things go bad, and he's threatened? What will he do?*

✦ ✦ ✦

The day he was set to leave, Luke tiptoed into my tiny bedroom in the cabin and woke me up before dawn. I crept out of bed in the dark, feeling the misty air, blinking my eyes to stay awake. I heard only a few bird calls. Otherwise, apart from the gentle surf, it was deeply quiet. Luke and I climbed the hill to the house, holding hands. Mom and Bubbe, wrapped in their bathrobes, were waiting in the kitchen to say goodbye. I hugged Luke tight, frightened now by what he might face.

He murmured, "Take good care of yourself, Pig."

"I will. You take care. I love you."

He slipped out the door. Dad followed.

I felt proud of Luke but held back tears as I walked toward the door. Mom and Bubbe were close behind me. We trundled down the few back stairs and waved as the car motor began to rumble. Dad turned on the car beams and drove off with Luke to the airport. Mom and Bubbe waited a moment before they shuffled back into the house.

I peered into the darkness at the empty space he'd left behind. In my pajamas and barefoot, I walked down the hill feeling the cool damp grass between my toes. I stopped outside the cabin to breathe and listen to the waves—to steady myself—before climbing back into bed and falling asleep.

✦ ✦ ✦

Because Luke had flown home to convince our parents about his decision to volunteer in Mississippi, he'd missed both main orientations held in Oxford, Ohio. Although most summer volunteers attended one of those orientations, there were shorter ones available for people who could not make it to Ohio.

On the plane to Memphis, Luke began to jot notes. During his stay at home, I had been unaware that, behind the scenes, he and Dad were having conversations of their own. Huddled together in Dad's small study upstairs, Dad had posed questions that Luke continued to ponder as he left for the orientation. The first entry of his summer diary began:

Left Providence Airport 7:15 on 2 July, '64.

My anxiety on leaving—Dad feels we are lambs being led to slaughter. [He heard that] Malcolm X threatens to bring guerillas and violence to Mississippi which would undo all we are striving for. Racial violence might contribute to Goldwater campaign [for president]. These were some of Dad's arguments—and of course "why don't you work for civil rights in Providence or San Francisco where it's safe?"

Mom may be sick [with worry], and this frightens me. I hate to contribute to anxiety which already exists at home.

It wasn't frivolous for Luke to be worried. Mom was sensitive, prone to disabling anxiety and depression. He continued writing: "I am sitting on the plane . . . and wondering what is old Luke getting himself into now?" So, privately, he did have doubts that he never revealed to any of us.

I know in hindsight that many other young northern volunteers experienced an identical rift with *their* parents. Like Luke, they had been raised to be idealistic, and their parents' resistance only strengthened their own resolve to go. The dissonance between what Luke had been taught by our parents and how they tried to dissuade him was probably provocation enough to convince him to go to Mississippi, despite any private doubts he may have had.

Like many other young volunteers, Luke was still in school and financially dependent on our parents. Gripped by fear, some parents prevented their offspring from volunteering by refusing financial support. Volunteers under twenty-one needed written parental permission. Like ours, however, many parents reluctantly came around to accepting their children's choices no matter how uneasy they felt. Luke was twenty-five and thus older than many other volunteers. Already seriously engaged in his career, the stakes were higher because of what he might lose, but he was determined to go. I suspect that Mom and Dad came to respect his steadfast sense of purpose, even if they were just resigning themselves to it.

"There's nothing we can do to change his mind anyway," Dad admitted grudgingly. "If we stand in his way, it's likely we'll sow conflict with him way into the future. We can't take that chance. It's not worth it."

Chapter 2

RECRUITMENT AND ORIENTATION

Once the Summer Project leaders decided to recruit white volunteers, they carefully planned their outreach.

Program Director Bob Moses cautioned potential volunteers, in the language of the day: "Don't come to Mississippi this summer to save the Mississippi Negro. Only come if you understand, really understand, that his freedom and yours are one."

The leaders realized that students from privileged families could afford to volunteer rather than seek a paying summer job. Recruiters targeted students at prestigious colleges and universities, including Harvard, Yale, and Stanford, the latter of which is where Luke first heard about the project. Volunteers were asked to bring money to cover not only the cost of food and necessities but also, if they could, an extra $500 to post bail in the likely event they were arrested. Of course, many students from public and less expensive schools, if able to raise funds, were eager to volunteer as well.

Among others, Martin Luther King Jr. visited Stanford in the spring of 1964. Although he was not involved in planning the project, King spoke to a large crowd of students. "In the Mississippi power structure, justice has no meaning. . . . Civil rights issues cannot be resolved from within the state; help must come from the outside."

Luke was in the audience. He was eager to respond to the call.

Beyond financial considerations, there was another reason that project leaders wanted to recruit volunteers from prominent families. Unfortunately, they knew that the national news media was much more likely to pay attention to what privileged young whites were up to rather than segregated Black youth in impoverished communities. Volunteers provided names of their hometown and college newspapers. Project leaders planned to send news releases to these papers—to make sure they published stories about what their local youth were encountering in Mississippi. All summer long, almost daily, Luke would send letters to Stanford to report on his experiences. Going forward, local newspapers around the country began to pay attention, as well as many individuals, including my parents and me, along with the parents, siblings, teachers, and neighbors of other volunteers. Movement leaders anticipated that, during the coming months, a media spotlight would shine into the dark corners of Mississippi where before there had been only ignorance and neglect.

✦ ✦ ✦

Freedom Summer was Program Director Bob Moses's brainchild. For the past two years, he had been working with persistence, and at great personal risk, on the voter-registration drive in Mississippi. Voter registration was the key, but he and his fellow field-workers were not achieving the momentum they needed to truly make a difference. In segregated Mississippi, white people fiercely resisted the effort to register Blacks. They were determined to maintain their supreme political power by any means. In proposing the massive effort of Freedom Summer, Bob Moses advocated strongly for bringing in northern Black and white volunteers. The sheer number of people involved would matter; however, the issue of asking whites to come join Blacks in Mississippi on the frontlines of the civil rights movement was very controversial.

Other Black field-workers voiced persuasive concerns: "Why do we need whites here to help us? Won't they try to take over and tell us what to do, the way they always do? Isn't this *our* struggle?"

Their worries were heartfelt and real. They knew it was not going to be easy to meld whites into the work they had already devoted themselves to doing on their own.

There were several open questions: How would large numbers of whites react to life in Mississippi, living in the homes of their courageous hosts and learning to follow the lead of Black field-workers? Would they help the cause or not? How would Blacks react to white volunteers who knew almost nothing about their culture or the lives they lived? The summer ahead promised to be a grand experiment in fostering social change and democracy.

✦ ✦ ✦

Disembarking from the plane in Memphis, Luke discovered he was in the company of another white volunteer, Mason Freeman Cocroft, who went by his middle name. He was twenty-two years old, grew up in Providence, Rhode Island, and had graduated from college at Yale less than a month before. His name, Freeman, struck Luke as particularly apt. The two would become fast friends and roommates through the summer.

At the orientation, the trainers were Black field-workers who had already been busily setting up community centers in Mississippi and laying the groundwork for the Summer Project. They repeatedly reminded Luke and the other northern volunteers that their African American coworkers must always be the ones in charge. Developing Black leadership was an essential goal. To show proper respect, whites would need to learn to hold back their own opinions, no matter how much expertise they thought they had. They needed to remember that the bravery the northern volunteers might demonstrate during the summer would inevitably be far overshadowed by the courage of their African American coworkers and hosts. It was one thing to visit Mississippi, quite another to live there. After all, white northerners could easily return to their lives of privilege any time they chose, but their Black brothers and sisters in the movement could not. One of the white volunteers, Sally Belfrage, observed, "The struggle was their life sentence, implanted in their pigment, and ours only so long as we cared to identify."

During the orientation, Luke kept running notes in his diary and scribbled daily letters he sent for safekeeping to his close friend and fellow Stanford medical student Art Zelman. "Dear Art," he wrote, "the letters I send you are the truth as I see it."

Wanting to document what he was learning, Luke's first entries read like a report:

> We are going to Mississippi for a cause and Mississippi doesn't believe in causes. We are going to Mississippi for one thing— because men and women have used other men and women as objects to get what they want.
>
> At the orientation they emphasized the dangers and tried to frighten away the less committed.

The trainers shared personal stories with the new volunteers in order to bring home the dangers.

> There was a terrifying story by a civil rights worker about being surrounded by men who threatened to kill him. He told how he saved himself. He felt one man was wavering and concentrated discussion on him.
>
> Eric described being hit in jail: "Talk to them. They are curious about you." He didn't jump when struck at, and this demonstration of trust for the man who threatened him led to friendship.

During the workshops, volunteers were taught essential non-violent techniques. "We learned how to fall and protect our vital organs." The trainers also raised difficult practical issues regarding guns and nonviolence.

> [We were] told not to ever strike back: "You can destroy the entire movement by weapons—destroy faith of Negroes in the movement."
> . . . [And yet] it's not our job to preach nonviolence—i.e., don't encourage Negroes to give up their guns.

So, Blacks outside of the movement would keep their guns for protection and self-defense, but no civil rights workers could have them. Staying nonviolent was of paramount concern.

Although Luke was writing to Art, we hadn't heard from Luke yet at home. Our parents knew he was busy. They assumed he would make a collect call home once he was settled in Mississippi. They always placed great value on not being intrusive and thus took a hands-off approach. Besides, Luke had clearly asserted his independence. Their arguments against his going hadn't worked out so well. Only a few days had passed since he'd left, but still we were waiting on tenterhooks for any news.

Luke's first letter to Art took a more personal turn toward the end: "We felt very close to each other—the way soldiers must feel when they are about to go to the front lines." And he admitted feeling trepidation. "I'm getting into a rougher situation than I had bargained for."

In addition to training in nonviolence, volunteers learned freedom songs. Luke wrote: "We sang We Shall Overcome with more feeling than I've ever heard the song sung. It was hard to sing We are not afraid but for a minute or two I was not very afraid." These songs became a vital resource for the volunteers and for all the civil rights workers since they helped build a sense of solidarity.

Freedom Summer activists at Western College for Women, Oxford, Ohio, singing "We Shall Overcome" before boarding the bus bound for Mississippi. Photo by Ted Polumbaum. Ted Polumbaum/Newseum Collection.

There were songs to capture every emotion, and words changed to suit the circumstances of the moment. Gail Falk, a fellow volunteer who would later become a close friend of Luke's, remembers that at her orientation:

> I learned a whole new way of singing. The staff, in their bib overalls, didn't so much teach us as they did let the music pour out of their beings into ours.... I started to sing with my body and my heart, singing at the top of my voice yet losing my individual voice completely in a blend of all the voices. I think the actual moment I joined the movement was the moment that night I opened my mouth and sang too.

Leaving the orientation, volunteers were handed their assignments, either to do voter registration or teach Freedom School. Luke would be a Freedom School teacher in Meridian, the city where Mickey Schwerner and James Chaney had lived and worked and where twenty-year-old Andrew Goodman had arrived as a new volunteer just one day before disappearing. Luke was stunned.

Meridian—ooogh—not Meridian—that's where Schwerner came from—what? We're going there to take Mickey's place at the Community Center—good grief—

What will my parents think of that?

We are going to restore the Community Center which was closed down after their disappearance. There is a strong obligation for us to do a wonderful job for Schwerner.

As the search for the three missing men stretched on, it was becoming more evident that they had been murdered. No wonder Luke waited to be in touch with our parents. He still hadn't contacted us. He must have been thinking, *When they find out, they'll go ballistic. How can I possibly break this news to them?*

Chapter 3

A JEWISH THREAD

As Luke and Mickey Schwerner were close in age and background, Luke identified with him as a kindred spirit. Born in May 1939, four months before the outbreak of World War II, Luke was six months older than Mickey. Both were secular Jews raised in the shadow of the Holocaust. Mickey and his wife, Rita, had come to Meridian six months earlier to set the stage for Freedom Summer. Mickey understood it was inflamed hatred that had led to the Holocaust in Europe and the murder of his relatives there. He hoped the civil rights movement would give him a way to prevent the spread of hate. Luke shared this hope and aspired to live up to the example Mickey had set.

All four of our grandparents had immigrated to the United States around the turn of the century. They came from a region ruled by Russia in northeastern Europe, known as the Pale of Settlement, where Jews were allowed to live (in what is now Lithuania and Belarus). Mom's mother, our beloved Bubbe, grew up with her brothers and sisters in a forlorn rural shtetl situated at a minor market crossroads. Although girls were not supposed to be educated, her father taught her to read Yiddish. With delight, she read Yiddish translations of Leo Tolstoy's novels out loud. At fourteen, she made the journey to the United States with her twelve-year-old brother, Abe, in tow.

In her stories, she painted a vivid picture of their trip: There they were, just the two of them grasping each other's hands and sobbing on the ship. They refused to sleep apart despite regulations that kept boys and girls separated. Because no one could force them apart, they were finally allowed to stay together. When telling us this story Bubbe looked triumphant. She straightened up, slightly lifted her chin, and beamed.

For us children, Bubbe was our main link to the culture of Judaism. The kitchen was her domain. She cooked most of our meals, often traditional, peasant Jewish dishes. The scents still linger of chopped chicken livers, dill pickles she brined herself, beet borsht, chicken soup with matzo balls or kreplach, tender brisket, and buttery pan-fried blintzes stuffed with cottage cheese and piled high with sour cream. She spoke with a heavy accent, unwittingly lacing her speech with Yiddish words.

When Mom was a child, Bubbe's accent was embarrassing. Once, when Bubbe surprised her by coming to school, she pretended not to see her. *That's not my mother*, she wanted to say to her friends at the time, but it became a sorry source of regret for her later. Becoming assimilated and speaking English correctly were of great importance to Mom, but she was torn. She knew she should be loyal to family. In that instance, she had breached the bond. At the same time, Mom's attention to speech and language served her well. Raised in poverty, she achieved a full four-year scholarship, studying English literature at the University of Chicago.

Bubbe's background was Hasidic, which meant she'd been raised with dancing and singing. Being open-minded, she adapted easily to change, and her views of the world kept broadening.

Dad's parents were Conservative Jews. They met here, in the United States, but both had come originally from the bustling market town of Eishyshok, now in Lithuania, which boasted a rich history of Jewish scholarship. Growing up in Brooklyn, Dad had spent hours in Hebrew school, which prevented him from playing outdoors like the other neighborhood boys he envied.

He rebelled and became an atheist and a nonpracticing Jew. In science, Dad found a reprieve from superstitions that he saw as a constant part of his parents' world. Observing the natural world was another source of solace. Combining these two boyhood passions led him to become a doctor.

Although Dad did not value traditional Jewish observance, he bent to Mom's wishes when Luke approached the age of thirteen. We were living in California at the time, and Luke prepared for his Bar Mitzvah at a synagogue in Berkeley. Luke complained about having to learn Hebrew by rote, and Dad listened. After the Bar Mitzvah, Dad decided to ban religion altogether from our home.

When we later moved to Rhode Island, Mom and Bubbe made it a habit to dress up and sneak off on High Holy Days, just the two of them, to attend synagogue in the city of Providence. At home on these occasions, Bubbe baked tasty treats like rugelach and mandelbrot. For us children, then, there was culture but not religion. Eating Jewish foods, hearing Yiddish spoken, telling Jewish jokes, and sharing family stories defined the scope of our exposure to Judaism.

✦ ✦ ✦

Like Mickey and many other secular Jews his age, Luke thought deeply about the Holocaust. I remember when he was living at home while attending college, and I was an impressionable teenager.

Sitting around the kitchen table, he would pose probing questions. "How would you act, Pig, if you were in the Holocaust and they were leading you to the gas chamber? Would you obey and go along as you were told? Would you stay in line, or would you fight back?"

"Jeez," I replied stalling for time.

"I'd fight. I know I would," he continued, "and although that wouldn't save my life, I wouldn't go quietly. I'd try to grab one of their guns. I'd make a scene. Those guards—what they're doing is wrong and I'd want them to know it and pay for their crimes—even if I only got one of them or none. It's important to stand up for what's right, for justice."

What an awful question to think about! Had our grandparents stayed in the Old Country instead of coming to America, they would have been tortured and killed by Hitler's army and the local collaborators, their neighbors. Our parents too . . . maybe a baby Luke . . . I really didn't want to think about it.

But Luke had heard about a woman in one of the concentration camps. They say she began to dance when she was in line going to the gas chamber. She was naked like everyone else, and her head was shaved, but they couldn't stop her from beginning to dance on her own as if she really heard music. She was shot by a guard.

"She was a hero," Luke said, "because she didn't follow orders like the others."

✦ ✦ ✦

Luke asked me many other kinds of questions in those years when he was going to college and living at home. He was eager to discuss current events, and each week, with the arrival of *Newsweek*, he would choose a few short articles to read aloud. I learned to guess the tenor of topics by paying close attention to his changing facial expressions and his tone of voice. Whenever he read about the civil war in Laos (prelude to the war in Vietnam), he frowned, slowed down, and his voice dropped to a lower register. The pace quickened and he became animated whenever he read about the sit-ins happening in the South. They had begun in 1960 when I was thirteen and Luke, twenty-one. He admired the brave students who were sitting-in at segregated lunch counters and facing, with great dignity, the wrath of horrified whites.

Inspired by the sit-ins, my brothers, Luke and David, came up with a running joke. It related to our being Jewish in the WASP neighborhood of Plum Beach where we were viewed with suspicion as outsiders. The three of us agreed that we needed to pull off a "swim-in" of our own at the Plum Beach Club down the way. This private club had a restricted membership, which didn't include us. Whenever we stood on the rocky beach at the bottom of the hill below our house, we could easily spot the club. It sat on an inviting wide stretch of white sand. My brothers had decided we would swim there. That was the easy part, but we also needed to consider the next steps.

"OK, Pig, what do you want your sign to say?" Luke asked with a smirk.

David squinted and mused aloud, "When we're swimming over there, how can we hold our signs up in the air to keep them dry? What do we do?"

And then always came the punch line catapulting the three of us into raucous laughter: "How do you think they'll react?!"

The antics were funny, but the underlying story was not. My brothers probably created the joke to protect me. It was my story, and they understood how badly it made me feel. It had all occurred three years earlier after our family had moved from Providence into our house in Plum Beach. We moved in 1957, at the end of September. Since most neighbors were summer-only residents, their houses stood empty, like stark sentinels with blank eyes. Months passed. I explored the deserted yards. Many of my fifth-grade classmates at school were Navy children who lived on the base, sequestered in a world of their own. I longed for a girlfriend.

Realizing my plight, Dad bought me a pinto pony who arrived in March, about a month before my eleventh birthday. I named him Shawnee. We turned the garage into a makeshift barn. Stacks of hay bales lined the walls, and a garbage can held his oats. I spread straw on the floor of Shawnee's stall. Lugging pails of water out to him in the mornings, scooping manure after school, the sound of his munching, his warm fur, and the mixture of tangy smells were comforting. The two of us spent hours wandering through meadows and woods and along the rocky coast. Riding Shawnee

Julie (age eleven) and Shawnee. Photo by Herman Kabat, from a family album. Courtesy of the author.

bareback gave me a feeling of freedom. I often used the time to memorize songs and poems or make up ones of my own. I would sing and recite out loud to the rocking rhythm of his walking gait and the repetitive sound of the waves.

It was Luke who had first introduced me to serious poetry and classical music two years earlier, when I was nine years old. He was excited about courses he'd been taking in poetry and music appreciation. True to form, Luke wanted to share what he was learning with someone who would listen.

Shawnee and our dog, Jazzy, were good companions for outdoor adventures. At home, Luke helped to fill the gap. He was good human company. But still I hungered for a friend my own age.

When summer began, I felt very lucky to meet Judy Atkins with her beautiful long nose, inquisitive blue eyes, and brown hair. Her grandparents on both sides lived in Plum Beach, and she was moving back and forth between their homes for the summer. We shared a love of books and began playing imaginative games, forming a merry Robin Hood band with some of her cousins and friends. Before long, the girls invited me to the Plum Beach Club. After my first day there—swimming, building sandcastles, eating hot dogs, and lounging on the beach, I was excited to return. Judy showed up in our yard a day or two later, and I raced out to greet her, but she slowed down with her eyes cast down. When she halted, she was fidgeting and biting her lip.

She began speaking softly, "The mothers got together and decided. . . ." She hesitated awkwardly and squinted before blurting out, "They say you should only come down to the club three times a summer. Otherwise, they say, it'll cause too much of a stir."

I stepped back, transfixed like a deer caught in car headlights, confused. *Too much of a stir?* Without saying anything, I turned and ran into the house, shaking.

This was my rude introduction to anti-Semitism. Later, there were incidents. One crisp fall morning, I stepped out as usual on my way to feed Shawnee before school but leapt back bug-eyed. A pair of oddly glistening chicken legs with bony feet stared up from the doorstep.

I wondered, *Who had left them, and* why? But I knew what they meant to me. They signaled someone shouting: *You Jews eat lots of chickens! You're like this bird. You, too, deserve to be dismembered and left to rot. Do you like this special gift I brought for you?*

Another time, when Mom and I were driving down the hill toward home, a boy glared at us, pointing both his thumbs down. I assumed I knew what he meant too. *What's he got against me? I don't even know him,* I thought, feeling like an outcast.

Despite these challenges, Judy and I remained close friends. We kept playing together, reading books and poetry, and by the next year, she and her mother moved in year-round with her grandmother. She still went back and forth between her grandparents' homes, but at either one, she lived just a short distance away. The two of us were in the same classes at school and became inseparable.

Luke, of course, was always a comforting presence at home. He and David kept up their joking. I became rebellious and made it a habit to ignore all the No Trespassing signs posted around the neighborhood. *After all,* I thought, *who gets to make the rules? And who says so?* Both of my brothers encouraged this newfound sense of independence and my questioning authority.

These sporadic episodes of prejudice were not the systematic oppression experienced by African Americans. They don't compare in scale or impact, of course, but they were painful nevertheless.

Reacting to these incidents, I welcomed my brothers' running joke. As we sat around the kitchen table, it was reassuring to know they cared.

"So, what's your sign gonna say?" David would ask, raising his eyebrows and glancing at me askance.

We'd crack up. Just picturing the disruption that our protest could cause at the Plum Beach Club felt liberating.

Why not? I thought. *Why not stir 'em up?*

✦ ✦ ✦

How had our neighbors learned we were Jewish? Perhaps it was during our first spring when the next-door neighbors invited Bubbe over for a luncheon. Our gentle grandmother was completely unworldly and came from a humble background. She looked very Jewish and spoke with a heavy Yiddish accent. Needless to say, Bubbe was never invited back. After that, Mom barely let her out of the house except to shop for groceries or when the two of them escaped to Jewish neighborhoods in the big city of Providence.

Then again, our neighbors may have heard that Dad saw patients at Miriam, the Jewish hospital in Providence. Since there was no one we could ask, we surmised that the owners who sold us the house must have harbored anger at their neighbors, which led them

Bubbe at the dining room table. Photo by Paul Shain.

to break the taboo, a silent agreement NOT TO SELL TO JEWS OR BLACKS. Anger may have stiffened their resolve because how else could we explain why they immediately accepted Dad's first offer, which was only half their asking price? All we did know for sure was that the house had sat on the market for a few years, and they had never received a previous offer. Dad bought the house on the hill with its acre of sloping land "for a song." Little did he know the previous owners were setting a trap not only for their neighbors but also for us. Feeling like an outcast led me to spend more time with my big brother Luke than I might have otherwise. And this experience may have prompted Luke to take me further under his wing. It brought home not only the fact that we were Jewish but also the pervasive, cutting cruelty of prejudice.

Chapter 4

A MORAL COMPASS

Luke found many other stories about current events that were filled with moral dilemmas and ripe for discussion. He wanted me to understand that the question of how you can tell right from wrong can be complicated. You need to look at the circumstances, but there are also principles that can serve as guideposts.

One day he asked, "So, Pig, what do you think about capital punishment and the death penalty?"

I looked up at him blankly but quickly remembered the Chessman case we'd been following in the news.

Caryl Chessman was a prisoner at the San Quentin Prison in California, accused of being the "Red Light Bandit," a robber who had kidnapped two women. That was a really awful crime, but many people believed he had changed in prison and shouldn't be executed. He had lived on death row for twelve years and wrote four books. At the end—so horrible, his execution in a gas chamber was a mistake.

Luke recounted, "Earlier when Chessman was about to be executed, he'd always gotten a reprieve at the last moment. There was supposed to be one this time. The judge's secretary called the prison to say there was a stay and they should hold off, but the phone lines were busy." Luke grimaced. "Can you believe it? By the time she got through, it was too late."

He turned to look me in the eye. "So, how can it be wrong for a man to kill someone—as it says in the Ten Commandments—but right for the government to do? The government represents us, the people, and we're not supposed to kill. Isn't it just a barbaric form of revenge?" Luke shook his head, perplexed. "Two wrongs don't make a right. Remember that Pig."

Luke's style of questioning made a vivid impression on me. Looking back, I see that, by asking these tough questions, Luke felt himself to be part of the wider world, and he was inviting me to feel part of it too. He was also honing his talents as a teacher by asking me open-ended questions that encouraged critical thinking. Through our interactions, he learned how to engage and challenge a teenager, skills he would draw upon as a teacher at the Meridian Freedom School. Because he was always questioning and searching for context, I'm sure that when Luke received his assignment at the end of the orientation, he spent time thinking about Mickey Schwerner and his wife, Rita.

✦ ✦ ✦

The young couple had arrived in Meridian in January to help prepare for the Mississippi Summer Project. The entire project was administered through the Council of Federated Organizations (COFO). COFO was a coalition of national civil rights groups that agreed to coordinate their efforts in Mississippi to minimize political infighting. The most active groups that participated in COFO were the Student Nonviolent Coordinating Committee (SNCC), to which Luke belonged, the Congress of Racial Equality (CORE), and the National Association for the Advancement of Colored People (NAACP). CORE was the organization responsible for the project in Meridian and its surrounding territory. At all project sites, older local activists served as mentors for the new arrivals.

As a CORE field-worker, Mickey had opened the COFO office to serve as the headquarters in this eastern part of the state. It was housed on the second floor in a building on Fifth Street in downtown Meridian. Administrative offices coordinating voter registration were located next to the Community Center, which took up a large open space. It functioned as a magnet for children. Everyone marveled at how much all the children loved Mickey. They called him a big bear.

Mickey radiated a magnetic presence that drew others to him. James Chaney was one of them. Mickey had hired James as a local staff member, and he soon became Mickey's most reliable coworker.

According to his mother, Fannie Lee Chaney, James confided, "Mickey Schwerner—I never knowed a man on earth who could live like him. . . . Momma, that man got sense. . . . he came here to help us and I'm not going to let him do it by hisself. I'm going with him."

James was rather shy in public but full of antics at home. He had been a Freedom Rider as a teenager back in 1962, bravely sitting up front on an interstate bus to protest segregation. The Freedom Rides had begun the previous year in 1961. Thus, James was already active in the civil rights movement by the time Mickey and Rita arrived in Meridian.

Mickey and James had been scouting out spaces in rural areas surrounding Meridian in which to locate future Freedom Schools. Since James was Black, he could go places unnoticed, whereas a white person, like Mickey, would stand out. For several months, they had been negotiating with the Mt. Zion Methodist Church in Neshoba County and were hoping to open a Freedom School in the church.

Andrew Goodman, twenty years old, was the youngest of the three. He was a brand-new recruit from New York. In her memoir, his mother, Carolyn, wrote:

Then, in the spring of 1964, he stood in the doorway of my bedroom one afternoon with an earnest look in his soft brown eyes and said, "Mom, I'd like to go to Mississippi." . . . [I realized] the reasons why part of me so wanted Andy to stay were the same reasons he wanted to go. . . . My son wanted to be a beacon of light in the heart of darkness. How could I deny him?

Mickey and James were busy teaching at the second orientation held in Oxford, Ohio, when they met Andy among the volunteers.

Disturbing news reached James and Mickey from Neshoba County. On June 16 the Ku Klux Klan had targeted the Mt. Zion Methodist Church. Klan members assaulted three parishioners during the afternoon and returned under cover of night to torch the church, burning it to the ground. Mickey and James decided to investigate, and they asked Andy to join them. Leaving the orientation one day early, they drove through the night, arriving in Meridian in the wee hours of the morning. That afternoon, the three young men drove out to Neshoba County. Andy was known to be alive in Mississippi for less than twenty-four hours.

As Mickey Schwerner was beloved by everyone, his absence created a huge gap. No one could replace him, but Luke and his new friend, Freeman Cocroft, accepted the responsibility of taking up his cause. Leaving the orientation, Freeman put it this way: "At Memphis, Luke and I were told that when Mickey was alive, the Meridian Community Center was the . . . place . . . where Negro kids smiled. It was our desire to see them smile again and keep them smiling as often as any human being could ever be expected to smile." They set out for Meridian along with others to pick up the pieces and to carry on Mickey's fight for freedom.

Chapter 5

MERIDIAN

Throughout the spring of 1964, community centers like the one Mickey started in Meridian popped up around the state. Word spread quickly to African American teenagers and children. Among them were the Thompson sisters of Meridian who belonged to a large, tight-knit family of nine children with seven girls and two boys. Andreesa, the second oldest, was seventeen at the time.

In a conversation with me fifty years later, she recalled: "We were hearing about Freedom Summer before it began because of the authorities. They kept saying, 'We *got* to get ready for those Freedom Riders comin' to start trouble down here. Those communist agitators.'" Her voice took on a mocking tone. "They'd say, 'We don't know *why* they're comin' to Meridian! *We* have our Negroes under control down here.'"

That's it, I thought. Under control . . . Andreesa's nailed it! She's managed to sum up the rationale for segregation and white supremacy in two troubling words.

Andreesa remembers how her sense of anticipation grew through the spring of 1964.

"I was kind of excited about it. I thought, I want to see some new faces and see what's going on. Our good friend Roscoe Jones came over to our house one day and said, 'Let's check it out. Let's see what's going on. We're gonna *learn* something.' He was always

Looking across Fifth Street at the COFO Community Center (second floor).
Courtesy of Gail Falk.

Ku Klux Klan poster found in
the men's room at a gas station
in Mississippi. © 1976 Matt
Herron/Take Stock/TopFoto.

Fifth Street view. Courtesy of Gail Falk.

saying that. 'We're gonna *learn* something!' *That* was Roscoe! So, at first, we all followed him down to the community center. We soon got the hang of it, and we really enjoyed it."

"Were you scared to go?" I asked.

She laughed. "I don't think I knew enough to feel unsafe. Somebody's having a good time, and I wanted to be in on it. That's all. I was curious."

I hadn't anticipated meeting Luke's former Freedom School students, including Andreesa and her sisters, when I went to Meridian in 2014 to celebrate the fiftieth anniversary of Freedom Summer. For me, the trip was a pilgrimage to follow in my brother's footsteps.

"Oh, Luke!" each former student exclaimed when we met, embracing me with a grin.

I was even more astonished to discover that two of the Thompson sisters, Andreesa and Dorothy, now lived in Albany, New York, close to where I lived.

About six weeks after the 2014 reunion in Meridian, we were back home in New York. Dorothy, Andreesa, and I went out to lunch. We chatted, marveling at the simple fact that we were sitting together. Then the sisters looked back fifty years to share memories of Freedom Summer.

Andreesa reminisced, "We got to know the volunteers, you know? And they were the first white people we ever met who would interact with you. When they did at first, I don't know if I was overwhelmed or was it curiosity—"

Dorothy cut in. "Down in Mississippi, white people were nice to you when you worked for them. I mean they would talk to you if you were their maid or something, but not when you weren't working for them."

"The volunteers were different. They would actually play with you and not call you names."

"Luke was so cute!" mused Dorothy, thirteen at the time and looking shy even now. "He had a face so like a child."

Andreesa agreed. "He was cute. Everyone thought so . . . a cute white boy. Luke would always just sit on the floor with us, cross-legged Indian style. All the kids wanted to be right there with him. They were *always* asking Luke questions."

I was curious. Before Freedom Summer began, what was it like for them to be Black children growing up in Meridian? Could they help me understand the world Luke was entering when he arrived?

So, I asked, "What are your first memories of segregation?"

Andreesa hesitated a moment, drew in a breath, and began in a calm voice. "Our mother would always say, 'If you go someplace, go with each other. Don't ever, ever go anywhere by yourself. Take Dorothy with you.' Wherever I'd go, she'd repeat that. 'Take Dorothy with you!' When you played in the street, Mom would be watching from the front porch. You didn't play in the backyard where she couldn't see you. And when it got dark you just stayed in."

She paused briefly and then continued at a faster pace. "You see, there was a boy in our neighborhood. He was older than us, about twelve years old when he wandered off by himself one day. We don't know why, he just did. In the afternoon, he knocked on a white woman's door. Maybe he was lost and asked for directions or for food because he was hungry. This woman invited him in and then asked him to wait while she got him something to eat from the kitchen. He was found in the street later. Dead. His parents were suspicious, so they asked the doctor. Poison was found in his body. Nothing ever came of it. There was nothing to be done, but we never went anywhere alone."

I was shocked. What could have possibly been going on in that woman's mind as she prepared his food? What kind of a monster would do this?

Dorothy chimed in softly. "A girl our age disappeared, and she wasn't found. If you would inquire about it, and then feel nothing's being done . . . If you go back to ask the police and authorities something about it, they'd get nasty."

"*Really* nasty," Andreesa added fiercely, "and you'd fear for your own safety. So, you would have to leave it alone."

Dorothy shook her head sadly. "They never found her." She gazed into the distance. Andreesa glanced tenderly across the table at her sister. "'Take Dorothy with you,'" she whispered. "Even today I hear that in my head. We're always together. I still find it hard to go out alone."

So, that was the undertone of ordinary life for a child growing up in Mississippi during the Jim Crow era. It was the world Luke would encounter when he came to live with a Black family and teach students at the Freedom School in Meridian.

Listening, I swallowed hard.

Part Two

MISSISSIPPI
FREEDOM
SUMMER

Chapter 6

EARLY DAYS

Luke scribbled notes into his diary while riding on the bus with Freeman from Memphis to Meridian.

Saturday, the 4th of July, the day of the signing of the Civil Rights Bill. . . .

Greyhound bus bound for Meridian. . . . Mississippi looks greener than I thought—and pretty as can be. . . .

It looks too calm and nice to be so violent a place . . . —funny red dirt—could be KuKluxers behind those dark trees—

Philadelphia [where the young men disappeared] looked ugly and mean to us and we were scared to get out of the bus when it stopped there—

I have a funny feeling as I write this diary that it might outlive me, and this is frightening. I have never thought so much about death. The cadavers at the medical school weren't me.

✦ ✦ ✦

Summer Project leaders anticipated that the presence of northern white volunteers could further inflame the dangerous situation in Mississippi. At the orientation, they had warned that Mississippi whites were experiencing a fear bordering on paranoia. Luke had jotted these notes in response:

> [Whites] feel they are fighting a lonely and noble battle. . . . Newspapers have made monsters out of us and have prepared people for months that invaders would come.
>   . . . After you leave, the Negroes who have sheltered you may suffer reprisals.

Thus, being a host and sheltering volunteers required an extra dose of courage.

Mr. Figgers invited Luke and Freeman to stay with him. He was a frail, kind father of ten grown children who now lived by himself. Luke was aware of the risk they posed to him: "I hate to endanger his life by staying at his house, but he is proud to be able to help in the fight for freedom."

Their bedroom was at the side of Mr. Figgers's tidy, small house and faced the street. Flowers clung to the walls outside and grew around the windows. "Free and I are sharing a bedroom. It is a friendly place and I know that I will be happy here this summer."

On their first morning, Luke awakened early, intending to make breakfast for Mr. Figgers. "When I awoke I heard a fizzy-type sound and it was bacon frying on a skillet. He beat me to the punch and had eggs and bacon, grits, coffee, etc. already prepared." Luke enjoyed getting to know Mr. Figgers, but he was also concerned.

> He grew up on a farm, had education to the 6th grade . . . served in WWI, likes to go fishing for catfish in the local crick. He has a good sense of humor.
>   He has a resting tremor and a Parkinsonian facies and gait. . . . I recommended that he visit a doctor and will try to get the name of a good neurologist for him.

Alas, Luke would soon learn that finding a neurologist for his host was unrealistic.

Mr. Figgers's yard. Photo by Gail Falk.

Dr. Polk was one of only two African American physicians in Meridian. The city had an overall population of roughly fifty thousand. These two doctors were expected to serve the entire Black community of twenty-three thousand. Despite being impossibly busy, Dr. Polk made time to meet Luke as soon as he could.

During their first visit, Dr. Polk explained, "It took me seven years to get hospital privileges in this area."

Clearly, if you were Black, cost was not the only hurdle to receiving good medical care. Under segregation, separate was anything but equal.

Mrs. Graham, one of Mr. Figgers's daughters, lived next door with her family. They shared the backyard with chickens and a garden. Like her father, Mrs. Graham bravely hosted a northern volunteer, Gail Falk, who would soon become Luke's close friend.

On their first Sunday there, her husband, Reverend Graham, asked that Luke and Free not attend his church because "the people were afraid that their church would be bombed." Dangers lurked everywhere.

✦ ✦ ✦

Luke and Free agreed that their priority was to reach out to the children. Luke wrote in a letter he sent to Art:

> Today was my first day on the job. About thirty kids spent the day with us. It was like a second childhood for me. I read *Babar, The King* to three little children who were hugged up beside me. They were sad when the wise old elephant Cornelius was caught in a fire.
>
> . . . I was a horse for the kids and gave them wild rides and they shrieked as I galloped around. I painted pictures of silly animals for the kids. "I want a blue hippopotamus," "I want a yellow giraffe," "I want a red monkey," were some of the requests.
>
> I have had a great time with the kids. We organized the books in the library. I taught them to sing.

"BUM PUM PUM" went the song he taught. This song, "Black and White," lists ways that colors interact to make our world possible because the "ink is black," "the paper white," and the "earth turns from day to night."

Luke relished getting to know the children. Three brothers lived across the street from the Meridian Community Center: six-year-old Lance Williams, whom Luke described as "scrappy as can be, [called] 5th Street Red because he hangs out on 5th Street"; Lenray Gandy, "a dreamer kid, always sitting in the corner with his eyes closed"; and the oldest brother, eleven-year-old Larry Martin, a close friend of Ben Chaney whose older brother James was still missing. These brothers played and hung out at the Community Center as often as they could. The youngest, 5th Street Red, clung

Lance Williams (5th Street Red). Photo by Bill Rodd. Used by permission of Thomas Whitney Rodd.

to whatever part of Luke's body he could reach, whether his hand, shoulder, back, arm, or legs.

The Thompson sisters were there too, of course: nine-year-old Patty, accompanied by her younger sister Gwen who "loves to ride around on my back like a horse" and by Dorothy who was thirteen. Their older sister Andreesa showed up often to play games and read to the younger children. She kept a close eye on her sisters.

Luke knew that the children's grief for Mickey and James was profound. Offering comfort, he helped them voice their fears and memories. He found it very disturbing to witness the abrasive reality of segregation that permeated every aspect of their lives. He wrote: "One of the workers, Lilly, is a 15-year-old girl . . . the daughter of a white policeman and a Negro woman. It is ironic that the father enforces laws that make slaves of his own children."

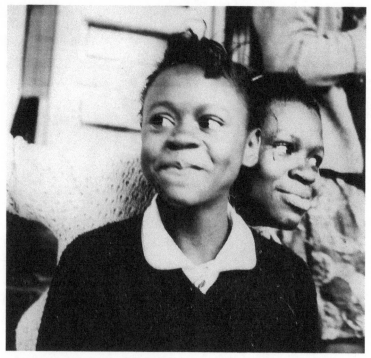

Patty and Dorothy, two of the Thompson sisters. Photo by Bill Rodd. Used by permission of Thomas Whitney Rodd.

As ugly as this was, it was not an unusual situation. Fathers of biracial children were most likely not to acknowledge them. These children lived in a white world that oppressed them.

There was Ed too. "Reading to the kids I was amazed to find a real child prodigy, an eleven-year-old Negro boy with glasses and an intense desire to learn physics. I decided to discuss atomic energy, fission and fusion, etc., but he already knew almost as much as I do about these subjects. When I made a little mistake about the speed of sound, he gently corrected me." Later, when Luke had the opportunity to meet Ed's mother, he discovered that she "is worried about him. She thinks he's a disturbed kid because he is only interested in atoms." Amazed by Ed's grasp of physics,

Luke with children at the COFO Community Center. Courtesy of Syrtiller Kabat.

Luke wondered: "How many fine Negro minds have never had the opportunity to learn? How many children like Ed will never go to college? The thought of him working as a janitor for white men makes me sick at heart." Deep-seated racist assumptions underlaid the regime of white supremacy and laid waste to so many lives. Luke felt protective of the children he was getting to know.

The COFO Community Center in Meridian quickly became an oasis for those who gathered there. Luke lovingly painted the scene:

> [The COFO headquarters] consist of a few rooms in downtown Meridian above a barber shop, near the Joe Louis Café, a taxi stand, and Henderson's Restaurant run by a 300 lb. man named Henderson of all things.

One room is for the COFO administrators, another is for voter registration and contains maps, etc., and the large room is for the kids. It has bookshelves on the walls, a green bench, a beat-up record player and a bunch of kids.

If you walked in on a typical day, you might find kids on the floor with paints and might hear music from the record player, rhythm and blues or freedom songs ("Well, have you been to the jailhouse? Certainly Lord"). You might see five or six kids, wrestling with Freeman and he would be smiling under a pile of them. I might be off in a corner with little Mary, Lance (5th Street Red), Ray, and some of the Wallace kids, reading a story—*Horton Hatches the Egg, Babar*, etc.

✦ ✦ ✦

Back at home in Rhode Island, it felt like forever before we heard from Luke for the first time. Over the phone, he gave us the news that he was in Meridian helping to reopen the Community Center that Mickey Schwerner had started.

"Oh my God!" whispered Mom, leaning into the receiver. "Lucien, are you sure you're safe?"

"Don't worry. I'll be OK." Static crackled the line. "I'm going to be teaching at the Freedom School. That's safer than the guys who go out in pairs, on their own, to do voter registration. I'm staying in the city here. I'm making friends, and the community looks out for us. Besides, the FBI has search teams covering every inch of territory around here."

Needless to say, Mom and Dad weren't reassured, but they tried to pretend they were.

When it was my turn to take the phone, I gushed, "Oh Luke! How is it there?"

His voice was warm and strong in response. "I love the kids down here. You would too, Pig. They're so brave and funny. I'm having a great time reading them stories—you know, the ones you loved as a kid—ones Mom read when you were little."

Standing at the entrance of the dining room, I glanced at Mom's books, novels, and literary criticism strewn around the room and overflowing the built-in bookshelves. Luke was right. Mom always had her head in a book and had passed on her love of reading to all of us. I was about to hang up the phone when Mom waved her hand, and I gave the phone back to her.

"Oh Lucien, dear, you're reading to the children? I want to help. I'll send you boxes of books, just let me know what stories you'd like." She paused a moment before adding, "We're really proud of you, darling. But we miss you terribly, you know."

After the phone call, my nerves were fluttering. Dad walked downstairs slowly.

Mom ran over to him, her arms outstretched, calling his nickname. "Hermtie! Will he be alright?"

As they embraced, I walked alone to the big windows on the front porch and gazed out at the bay. "He'll be OK," I said to myself over and over again. "I know he will. He's got to be."

◆ ◆ ◆

Unfortunately, it didn't take long for Luke and Free to witness the corrosive effects of racial hatred. They were taking a risk whenever they led the children outside the oasis of the Community Center for recreation. In a letter, Luke recounted:

In the morning we walked the kids to a nearby park and were followed by a man in a red truck. We asked him what he wanted, and he reached into his pocket. He pulled out a calling card [a social card printed with his name] and said, "Here, n----r lovers." We called the police and they arrived and questioned the man for a few minutes. After they left, the truck continued to follow us.

Another morning, Luke and Free were required to abide by the rules of segregation: "Two Negro boys that were coming with us to the community center had to pretend that they didn't know us and had to sit in the back of the bus. It is painfully embarrassing to have to reject your friends in such public situations."

Chapter 7

FREEDOM SCHOOL TEACHER

Luke's primary assignment, of course, was to teach at the Meridian Freedom School. Like all those involved, he was anticipating the first day of school with a mixture of eagerness and trepidation. Early in the morning on opening day, he paced back and forth near a concrete stairway that led up to the front door. All the teachers were wondering, *Will anyone come?*

The principal at segregated Harris High had issued a warning to his students, "If you attend the Freedom School, you won't be graduating from high school."

Although he himself was Black, Principal Barton's loyalty lay with the solidly white school board that hired him, not with his own community. Perhaps to protect his job or because he had internalized white supremacist talking points, he turned a blind eye to racial discrimination. He insisted that his teachers were not to participate in any civil rights activities and threatened his students with expulsion if they did.

And yet, according to Gail Falk, his stark warning went unheeded, as she wrote in a letter: "Well, from the first day, that building was full of children. More than 300 students were registered. Not all of them came every day. That was a huge part of the magic of it—children came because they wanted to and not

The Meridian Freedom School. Photo by Gail Falk.

because someone was making them." Out of sixty-four Freedom Schools located around the state, Meridian was the only one that had its own separate, dedicated building. This was a luxury. Formerly a Baptist seminary, the beige two-story brick building sat up on a grassy hill. The building had been neglected and vacant for a long time. Luke's first impression was that it was rather dark and forbidding, but the other volunteer teachers, who had arrived before he did, had already been hard at work cleaning it up and getting it ready.

Each Freedom School was a world unto itself. Because there was no central administration telling teachers what to do, improvisation was key. Guided by a loose set of goals, teachers were free to draw upon their own skills and respond to each of their students' interests and needs. Classes were kept small to ensure that students received individual attention. This was the stuff of Luke's fondest dreams—a school system set up to encourage a world of curiosity dedicated to learning. For the students, there was the added allure of being part of the civil rights movement, supporting the quest for freedom and equal rights.

As Andreesa attested, "We didn't just study history. We *made* history."

Students remarked on the sharp contrasts between their regimented, segregated school system and the freewheeling possibilities embraced at Freedom School. Students were encouraged to think, not regurgitate what they'd been told to say. Many found this very hard because they had never before been asked to think for themselves. Unlike the instructors at the segregated school, Freedom School teachers treated everyone as equals. History was taught differently too. Fifteen-year-old Robert in Gail's citizenship class described how history was taught in his regular school:

> You won't find in any Southern white school system where they teach Negro history.
>
> But at Negro schools, what do you have? Negro history?
> No! The white man's history. Why can't we learn of our [own] great-grandfather instead of Mr. Dick's [the white man's]?

In comparison, at Freedom School, students learned about their heritage. Citizenship was the only required class. In it, students discussed African American history and read books they'd never heard of written by famous Black authors, such as Richard Wright's *Black Boy*. They discussed how racism was used to maintain a *system of oppression*—dividing poor Blacks from poor whites in order to discourage them from working together for economic justice. Students learned about the struggle for civil rights and voting rights, and they grappled with the philosophy and tactics of nonviolence.

Although some of the students were open and inquisitive, Luke observed that many held back. "The kids have been deprived of mental stimulation and rather than being hungry for information, many have had the curiosity beaten down in them." But through exposure, they were changing: "Some are beginning to become excited by the things they learn at Freedom School and when a teacher has a response in class, you can see it in her smiling face."

The building was changing too. Luke reported, "We painted it [with murals on the walls] and brought such life to it that it became a beautiful place." With ingenuity, the teachers compensated for the utter lack of equipment and supplies. At lunchtime there was music. One of the teachers, Phil Corner, was a composer and musician. He would play, and kids danced the monkey. Women in the community cooked lunch for the teachers—dishing out hearty servings of home-cooked fried chicken, beans, potato salad, and cornbread. Savoring the aromas, Luke gobbled up his lunch, grateful for the women's gifts of food and their good company.

✦ ✦ ✦

Luke and Gail soon fell into a daily rhythm. Most mornings they walked the mile or two to school together through residential neighborhoods of modest wood-frame homes. Although most aspects of life in Meridian were segregated, surprisingly at the time, housing was not. On the way, as if they were on a checkerboard, Luke and Gail would pass by a row of white-occupied homes followed immediately by a row of Black-occupied ones. Their route took them through both poor and middle-class areas. They learned that on one white street, just a few blocks from their hosts' homes, lived a Meridian policeman named Lee Roberts. Some days, as they were walking, he would drive by very slowly in his police car and just stare at them. This was unnerving, but, despite it, walking back and forth to school during daylight hours felt safe. The walk provided a quiet time to plan for the day ahead.

Lenray Gandy. Photo by Bill Rodd. Used by permission of Thomas Whitney Rodd.

Luke wrote in his scrapbook: "He was a dreamer kid, always sitting in the corner with his eyes closed. He dreamed he was a scientist in a lab with magic & explosive chemicals. He was always bumping into reality—almost drowned in the swimming pool. When his brother 5th St Red went away for a week Len Ray [Lenray Gandy] became scrappy & outgoing—just like Red—and when Red came home, Len Ray became Len Ray again."

Free continued his daily work, teaching, reading, and playing with the young children at the Community Center. Watching Free, Luke felt wistful, wishing that he, too, had more time to spend with the young children. He admired the close bond Free was forming with them. He wrote:

In the morning as many as 15 kids come to our house to wake [Free] up. In the evening, after a long day's work, he tutors Floyd and Marshall and Carl.

Free loves the kids, and the kids love him. [He] buys the kids lunch every day.

Many of the young children at the Community Center came from poor families who experienced hunger. Luke found it painful to witness. "You can't believe how poor these kids are. The kids are hungry. They can't afford to eat lunch. . . . Len Ray [Lenray Gandy] once had a pair of shoes, but he lost them and goes barefoot as do many other kids. A little girl had so many holes in her dress that it hardly existed." The vaunted slogan of segregation, "separate but equal," was only a cruel, glaring taunt and a lie.

In contrast, most students at the Freedom School came well dressed and were, overall, more emotionally secure than the little children at the Community Center. The Freedom School teachers, of course, expected more mature conduct from the students of high-school age.

At Freedom School, in addition to citizenship class, there were remedial courses to help the teens catch up and enrichment classes in the arts and sciences to expand their understanding of the world. Enrichment depended on the strengths and knowledge each teacher brought. Composer Phil Corner taught music. Luke wrote about the school:

Inside [the building] there are infinite stories. A dance class with throbbing rhythmic music plucked out by Mark on a bass violin constructed with a washtub, rope, and stick, and Phil playing upon the flute. About 20 or so Negro girls with long arms and thin bodies move gracefully to the rhythm.

A biology class with a group of students gathered beside me. . . . I am telling them about planaria research or brain tumors . . . or so on.

Filled with conversation, speeches, and freedom songs, they offered
leaders and local residents a chance to speak and be heard. These
meetings provided the social glue needed to develop a palpable
sense of solidarity and sustain the mission of nonviolent resistance. Luke described the first one he attended: "I went to a large
meeting at the First Union Church. One speech was by Charles
Evers, brother of Medgar Evers who was shot . . . and as he talked,
the women in the crowd hollered, 'Freedom.' We sang freedom
songs and had a good time." In these meetings, singing helped
bridge the vast cultural gulf that existed between the northern
volunteers and their local comrades and hosts.

During another meeting at the end of Luke's first week, Mrs.
Polly Heidelberg, a local elder, rose to speak. Luke was more than
a little surprised. In fact, he was blown away by her spontaneous
oration, flabbergasted that a seemingly ordinary woman was
able to speak with such profound eloquence. He described her as
having "a touch of the poet."

Mrs. Heidelberg captured the language of the biblical cadences
she'd been hearing her entire life.

I have worked in your cornfield, I have nursed your babies, I have
cooked your food, I have picked your cotton, I have hoed, and all I
ask of you—to please let me be a free citizen to do the things that I
know is right. It is right for me to eat in a place if I have money to
buy your food, whatever you sell. Whether it is chicken or oysters
or greens or peas, I have a right to eat them. I raised it for you. I
cooked it for you. Then I don't have a right to sit down at the table
with you and eat? What a pity and a shame.

We afraid. We are even afraid to talk now. We can't ride the
buses. . . . We afraid to go to bed at night. We lookin' out the window. If a car stop we afraid somebody's goin' to hit us on the head
with a brick. We scared somebody gonna shoot in the windows. We
scared for our children to go to church.

Polly Heidelberg at the Meridian Freedom School. Photo by Mark Levy, Mark Levy Collection, Queens College/CUNY Rosenthal Library Archives.

Now what must we do to be free? Some peoples say we are free. Now what are we free of? We aren't even free to go to church on Sunday Night! They bomb our churches.

I intend to get my rights, but I intend to get my rights by doin' right. I will not give up. . . . We shall continue striving until every one of the Negro people is free.

Afterward Luke wrote that "listening to her was one of the great experiences of my life. . . . I think that if people in the North listen to her tell about her life in Mississippi . . . they will begin to appreciate what all this civil rights stuff is all about. I wish that

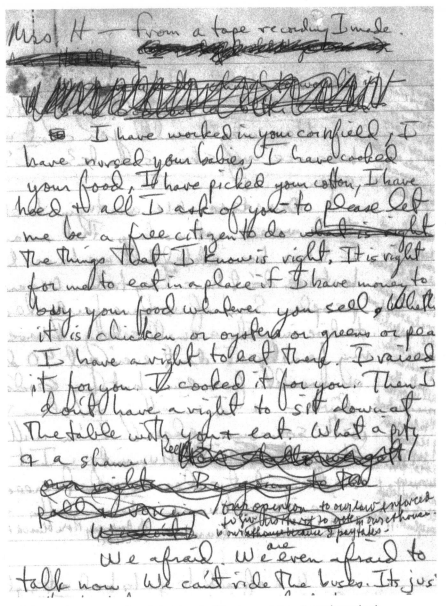

Mrs. H — from a tape recording I made.

I have worked in your cornfield, I have nursed your babies, I have cooked your food, I have picked your cotton, I have hoed & all I ask of you to please let me be a free citizen to do the things that I know is right. It is right for me to eat in a place if I have money to buy your food whatever you sell, whether it is chicken or oysters or greens or pea I have a right to eat there. I raised it for you. I cooked it for you. Then I don't have a right to sit down at the table with you + eat. What a pity + a shame.

We afraid. We even afraid to talk now. We can't ride the buses. Its jus'

Polly's speech: an excerpt from Luke's handwritten transcription. From the author's collection of Luke's private papers.

everyone could see and hear this wonderful woman. . . . She can move mountains with the power of her feelings." Later he visited Mrs. Heidelberg at her home and tape recorded what she said. He transcribed her words, copying them in his own handwriting onto yellow legal sheets of paper. The act of copying her words by hand helped him to absorb them.

On another occasion, Martin Luther King Jr. spoke at a mass meeting held at St. John Baptist Church. This time Luke was prepared. He brought along his tape recorder. Earlier in the day, Dr. King had visited Philadelphia, Mississippi. Luke wrote:

> He was very tired from a long hard day of speech-making, but he gave the people what they wanted to hear. He had been threatened with death if he came to Mississippi, and this was his response: "My life is no more precious than that of Medgar Evers [who was murdered]." . . . His words were simple but there was deep feeling behind the words, and everyone understood this feeling. His speech was punctuated by the cry "freedom!"

At the same meeting, Reverend C. T. Vivian spoke. He, too, was a national leader who worked for Dr. King's organization, the Southern Christian Leadership Conference (SCLC). Luke recorded and transcribed Reverend Vivian's speech.

> There comes a time when you start walkin' down the street toward dignity you can't turn back. It doesn't matter what you face. . . . We are not asking for the destruction of states' rights but we're asking for states to live up to their responsibilities. . . . Now because of men like Martin Luther King we've learned to love our neighbor. Now don't get me wrong. I'm not talking about getting halitosis from kissing Ross Barnett [prior governor of Mississippi]. I'm talking about the love that is willing never to harm another human being. . . . Love must lead the way.

Chapter 9

NONVIOLENCE 1

The question of how to base one's actions on love in the face of hatred was a prime topic of discussion. Throughout the summer, the volunteers found themselves in situations where they had to wrestle with difficult issues and question their assumptions, especially regarding nonviolence and racism. Luke, like many of his fellow summer volunteers, kept a running commentary in his notes. These diary entries carried extra weight and demanded further consideration. Luke would return to grapple with the nuances of their meaning time and time again.

> We will meet violence with nonviolence. This may be going out of style but is it going out of truth? For this is the only way to bring Black and White together after the walls are down.
>
> We are deeply angry over the hundreds of years of degradation and it isn't easy to be nonviolent, but we feel that the means will determine the ends.
>
> Are we trying to deny the white Mississippian his rights? We don't feel that he has a right to mistreat his Negro brothers.
>
> The Ku Klux Klan . . . has been arming with weapons stolen from an armory. How can we remain nonviolent in the face of such antagonists?

Negro population is armed to the teeth. . . . Discussion of the
Hypocrisy of being nonviolent when in fact being protected by
guns in Negro community. . . .

We role-played the various situations we might expect. . . .
Empty your pockets of sharp instruments or they will charge
you with carrying a concealed weapon. Don't order soup or hot
coffee as you may get it in the face. Ask for the menu or they may
charge you a higher price than listed. Don't talk back or you will
be charged with disorderly conduct. Above all—be nonviolent. If
someone hits you, do you know how to fall? Cover your head and
curl up.

Although they actively trained for violent confrontations and
taught nonviolence workshops at Freedom Schools, summer
volunteers were not allowed to go out to test the new Civil Rights
Act of 1964, which President Johnson had signed in early July, or
to engage in any other demonstrations. Project leaders had determined that voter registration, their priority, required a laser-like
focus. It would be foolish, they thought, to stir up controversy
in other areas. During the summer, it fell to other organizations
to plan local demonstrations. Holding back and not joining in
protests with their high school students and younger children
was very difficult for Luke and the other volunteers. It required
performing a balancing act—one that proved to be challenging.

Alas, there were other circumstances when volunteers found
themselves suddenly needing to confront hate with love. What
might at first appear to be an unremarkable situation could take
an unexpected turn. One afternoon, as he'd done many times,
Free took the children to Magnolia Park to swim. When he saw
Luke later that day, he hurriedly recounted what had happened.
Free also wrote an impassioned letter to his parents. Luke was so
shocked and disgusted by these events that he copied Free's letter
into his own diary and mailed a copy to his friend Art Zelman at
Stanford. Perhaps, as it had in the past, the act of copying the letter

by hand helped Luke to absorb and process what had occurred. This was the story Freeman told:

> Today we couldn't get the cabs to pick us up, and we decided to walk back to the COFO office. There were 34 kids and Ed and myself. While walking through the white neighborhood we could feel tension grow. . . . A man in a white Chevrolet was following us. . . . He called me a mother-fucking Communist. He called the kids n-----s, which they didn't like. . . .
>
> The man drove up as we were crossing the street. He hollered, "Don't worry little n-----s, I'm not going to run over him. I'm going to get him" (meaning me). The kids crossed the street, I began to cross. . . . The kids were hysterical when they saw me walking in front of that car. . . . They were crying and yelling and shrieking. He slowly drove up . . . and bumped me. At this point a policeman came over. I gave him my name and told him that this man had threatened to run me down.
>
> [A few cops gathered.] He denied everything, and they accepted his story. . . . One of the cops accused me of disorderly conduct because I disagreed with him. Some other whites came along and complained that we had trampled on their gardens. This was untrue. I was told to get into the police car and we rode down to the station. One charge was disorderly conduct. . . .
>
> The man had threatened to run me down and I was charged with obstructing traffic! The police sergeant looked at an ordinary kitchen knife, which was in my pocket. I had used it to cut the watermelon at the park. The knife had been in my shirt pocket where it could be seen by just about any fool, but I was charged with carrying a concealed weapon. Tomorrow I will have to go to court.

Free finished his letter, vowing:

> From the bottom of my heart, I love the kids here. To the best of my ability I will do what I ought to for them.

Yesterday I was ready to die when that car came at me. It was my feeling that no sacrifice was too much for the cause that would give little kids a decent chance to grow up with the self-respect they so justly and richly deserve.

Luke could only concur for he too loved the kids and was willing to sacrifice himself on their behalf. And like Free, he was horrified by the insanity and the injustice he was witnessing.

Chapter 10

A WORLD OF SONG

After their long work hours, Luke and his friends came up with a routine to help them relax. Most nights, around eleven o'clock, Luke, Free, Gail, and other young adults of the Graham family congregated in the backyard to watch the stars and sing songs. Both Luke and Gail had brought songbooks by Joan Baez and the Weavers with them. With Gail strumming on an old guitar and Luke playing solos on his harmonica, they sang old familiar folksongs, such as, "Gonna lay down my sword and shield / Down by the riverside . . . / Gonna lay down my sword and shield / And study war no more / I ain't a-gonna study war no more."

Luke and Gail often kept on singing after everyone else had drifted off to sleep. They were establishing a daily rhythm. Late one night, Luke scribbled into his diary: "It is strange that only a few weeks ago I was in Memphis and thinking of impending death in Mississippi. Now I am in Mississippi and am thinking only of life."

✦ ✦ ✦

Now Luke's phone calls home came every week or so. To me, the time of waiting felt much too long. In between calls, my parents and I combed through the *Providence Journal* and avidly watched the *CBS Evening News* with Walter Cronkite, searching for any

Luke and Lance (5th Street Red). Photo by Bill Rodd.
Used by permission of Thomas Whitney Rodd.

information we could find about what was happening in Mississippi, but it was slim pickings. What little we did hear was often grim. In contrast, when Luke called, he usually sounded upbeat, probably because he was making a conscious effort to distract us from worrying about him.

During our next phone call, Luke asked, "Why don't you send me some of the songs you've been writing, Pig? I'd like to hear them again, and I want to share them with folks here."

Many of these were peace songs I composed and sang with guitar. I had sometimes performed them at local coffee houses and even once onstage at the Boston Folk Festival when I was fourteen. On the phone, I asked Luke if he wanted me to include a few of his favorite old folksongs too, and he answered without missing a beat.

"Yeah! Sure thing."

I loved singing and sharing songs, whether they were my own or by others. Even then, in my late teens, I loved singing up in a tree behind the house. I'd climb the pungent-smelling cypress after dark, perch on a big branch, and hoist up my guitar with a rope.

When I was a little girl, Bubbe often called, "Julinka, come sing for me!"

Closing her eyes to listen intently, I'd watch her body relax and her face melt with pleasure. She sometimes told us a story I loved to hear about how her father sang when she was a child in the Old Country.

"His voice was so beautiful," she recalled. "People lined up outside the window. They came from all over just to hear him sing!"

Hearing that story, how could I not keep singing? In any circumstance that life might bring, why not sing?

Chapter 11

IN McCARTHY'S SHADOW

At the conclusion of his last phone call home, Luke noticed something strange. He wrote in his diary: "I heard noises which sounded like the wires were being tapped. I heard that this was a common practice in Mississippi and suspect that this may have occurred."

If Dad heard such noises, he would not have been surprised. He had heard the sounds of wiretapping ever since he'd been hounded during the McCarthy period in the early 1950s. At that time, Senator Joe McCarthy was fanning the flames of Cold War hysteria over suspected covert communist activities. The House Un-American Activities Committee (HUAC) was holding hearings. When Hollywood actors and directors refused to testify or name others as suspects, they found themselves blacklisted and cast out of the movie industry. Every American was routinely reminded to stay vigilant. The implication was this: You'd better look under your bed to be safe before you go to sleep at night. A communist just might be hiding there. After all, it was assumed, *they* were everywhere.

Some physicians in private practice who received the standard fee-for-service feared the example of the Kaiser health system. They may have thought it was suspicious. Doctors who work for Kaiser-Permanente are paid a salary. Doesn't *this* smack of socialism? And in the atmosphere created by McCarthyism, anyone could easily be tainted by association or harmed by innuendo.

Against this backdrop, Henry Kaiser Sr. may have been loath to arouse any further distrust.

It was late in 1953 when Dad's supervisor called him in. He wanted to discuss staff members whom Dad had hired.

"Are they above suspicion?" he asked, looking at Dad with piercing eyes. "If not, you need to fire them."

Dad was completely taken aback. He had surrounded himself with compatible colleagues, many of whom were politically progressive. Like him, they were neither activists nor revolutionaries. Dad came home to ponder his options. If he fired people, he could keep his job, but he asked himself, how could he fire someone who's done nothing wrong? They were his friends. He thought especially hard about one man who had numbers branded on his arm, reminding everyone, in a most painful way, that he was a Holocaust survivor. Sitting alone in his study, Dad closed his eyes and clasped his head in his hands, worrying. *How can I fire him after what he's been through? Hasn't he suffered enough?*

Dad reported back to work and met with his supervisor. Based on principle, he offered to resign instead.

These unfortunate events began to unfold when Luke was fifteen. Like every teenager, he was busy forming his own identity. This episode may help to explain why Luke, ten years later, was dumbfounded by Dad's reaction. He had every good reason to expect that his father would support his decision to go to Mississippi without hesitation. To Luke, Dad represented a man who had steadfastly stood by his principles.

Of course, Dad's resignation from his position was only the beginning of trouble. Those who suffered under McCarthyism often lost their jobs, sometimes their entire careers. They lost friends too. Many lives and webs of social relationships were upended. In the years that followed, our family life was disrupted in a way that affected Luke deeply and shaped his moral outlook.

For two years following his resignation, Dad was unable to land a job at another reputable institution. He started a private practice

Injured miner on a stretcher being loaded onto a Pullman train bound for the Kabat-Kaiser Institute in Vallejo, California, in 1948. Photo courtesy of Kaiser Permanente Heritage Resources.

in Berkeley but was not satisfied. He traveled to West Virginia for an interview only to discover that he was blackballed by members of the United Mine Workers of America. He had treated many injured miners under the Kaiser plan and felt crushed by that rejection.

Dad was surprised, then, when the governor of Rhode Island, Dennis J. Roberts, offered him a part-time job—to establish a rehab hospital and create a state-wide program for physical rehabilitation. Our family packed up, and we moved across country to Rhode Island.

In those unsettled years, Luke saw firsthand why it's important not to allow groups of people to be stigmatized. His sense of moral responsibility was evident in the letter he'd scribbled on a napkin, explaining his decision to volunteer in Mississippi. "I don't want to sit back while Negroes are being denied their rights—I don't want to 'let others do it' because it is <u>my</u> responsibility <u>too</u>."

Chapter 12

IN THE NEWS

Down in Meridian through the month of July, while Luke and his fellow activists were busy teaching at the Freedom School, registering voters, attending evening meetings, and singing, they were also staying attuned to any news they could find about Schwerner, Goodman, and Chaney. The local paper, the *Meridian Star*, carried news articles about searches in the area being conducted by the FBI, despite the fact that state and local officials still claimed the disappearance was all a hoax. Little by little facts were emerging.

On that fateful day in late June, when Mickey, James, and Andrew were not back in Meridian by 4:30 p.m. as planned, Sue Brown, the CORE worker who was waiting for them in the office, feared something was amiss. For civil rights workers out of the office, the afternoon phone check-in was a sacred ritual. She began calling the FBI, desperately pleading for help, but the FBI refused, claiming it was a local matter. One can only ask: What might have happened differently if federal authorities had intervened?

The day after their disappearance, when their still smoldering car was discovered in a swamp, supporters around the country mounted protests and held sit-ins at federal buildings. Rita Schwerner, Mickey's wife who was on her way back to Mississippi from

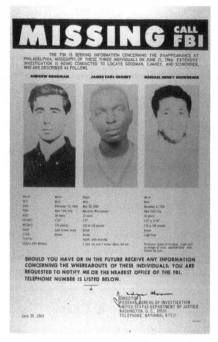

FBI missing poster of Andrew Goodman,
James Chaney, and Michael Schwerner, 1964.

the second Oxford orientation, spoke out boldly and pressured
President Johnson to expand the federal government's role in
finding the men.

As Rita later testified, "My husband believed very strongly in
security precautions, such as phoning in one's whereabouts, and
on several occasions, I heard him reprimand others who did not
call in to the office when they were supposed to . . . given the
opportunity, he certainly would have called in."

Media attention galvanized the nation. Attorney General Robert
Kennedy responded by asking the FBI to investigate. However,
even as FBI Director J. Edgar Hoover increased the number of
agents in Mississippi tenfold, he reassured white Mississippians
that the FBI would not give "protection" to civil rights workers.

In the weeks since then, FBI agents and sailors from a nearby naval air station continued scouring the woods, swamps, and rivers around Neshoba County where the three men had disappeared. In these searches, they uncovered the remains of at least eight others—African American men who had been lynched—unnoticed by the wider world. This was the tragic reality of segregated Mississippi.

For Luke and his fellow volunteers, the disappearance of the three young men, and questions about it, were part of the daily fabric of life, coloring all their experiences. James Chaney's younger brother, Ben, attended Freedom School, and the volunteers also became friendly with his sisters, Barbara and Julie, and with his mother, Fannie Lee, who was one of the women who cooked them lunches. Within the community, memories of Mickey and James were constant companions, and the atmosphere of shared grief was palpable.

✦ ✦ ✦

Meanwhile in Rhode Island, in response to Luke's request, I was busy recording a tape of my songs. I attended the Newport Folk Festival, and Pete Seeger was there. His enthusiasm was infectious as always, and he had all of us in the audience singing along and harmonizing with abandon. Years before, when I was twelve, Luke had taken me to my first Pete Seeger concert. I decided to include Pete's rendition of "Ecclesiastes" on the cassette tape I made for Luke because I knew it was one of his favorite songs. "All things have their time . . . a time to be born, and a time to die" begin the Bible verses on which the song is based.

In late July, Luke called from Mississippi to say he was glad to have the tape, played it often, and shared it with the kids at the Community Center. In this small way I, too, participated in Freedom Summer when my voice rang out in the faraway community that Luke was embracing.

✦ ✦ ✦

In early August, just over a week after he had played at the Newport Folk Festival, Pete Seeger came to Meridian as part of his
Mississippi state tour of Freedom Schools. On August 4, he gave
a concert at Mt. Olive Baptist Church. Luke and Gail were in the
audience along with about two hundred people. Among them,
seated toward the back of the church, were several white men with
short-cropped hair wearing dark suits and ties. Their presence
was curious, but the community was aware that FBI agents were
combing the area looking for clues as to the whereabouts of the
missing young men.

Gail wondered, *Maybe they've decided to come join us in singing
after a day of searching.*

Pete had already gotten everyone singing along with him and
enjoying the music when, at the end of a song, someone walked
up and whispered into his ear. Pete sang a couple more songs and
then made a sober, devastating announcement.

Luke's hand was shaking as he wrote the next entry into his diary.

On Tuesday night I heard the news that Chaney, Mickey, and
Andrew had died. Their bodies had been found . . . I was sitting in
front of Chaney's aunt at a concert given by Pete Seeger when he
made the announcement. She looked at me with startled eyes. "Is
it true?" she asked me. "I am his mother's sister. I am his mother's
sister."

My first feelings were shock for I have been close to those who
loved them. They insisted that the boys were missing and found
comfort in hope. I have known intellectually that they were dead,
but emotionally I refused to believe it.

I have been working in the Community Center that Mickey
built, and he lives there still in the minds and hearts of the kids.
They remember the story hour and how he played Frankenstein
with them and many other things. So I feel that I know Mickey too.

He worked so hard that sometimes he didn't eat for days and when I go to Henderson's for lunch, I can feel him saying, "Luke, get back to those kids—we've got work to do—there's freedom to be won." We wanted him to live and so we insisted that he was alive.

My next feeling was anger—I wanted to go to Neshoba County—I wanted to let Sheriff Rainey and his fellow murderers know that these murders will not turn us back. I felt that we must react immediately while people were feeling the full impact of horror and indignation. It is sad that people forget so fast. I wanted time and life to stop for a while and for all men to think about these boys—what they lived for and what they died for.

We sang freedom songs at the Seeger concert and I felt a deep sadness as I sang. I kept thinking that Mickey and Chaney and Andrew will never sing again. Listen to the words of the song: "They say that Freedom—Is a constant dying." As we sang I listened hard to these words and I forgot about the pretty melody and rhythm and felt sick—The price of freedom is so dear.

After a short hiatus, Luke returned to his diary. "The last few days have been so packed with life and the anguish of death that I feel incapable of adequately describing them. . . . Polly Heidelberg told me today with tears in her eyes that she couldn't sleep all night. She said, 'the most high, the most humble, the most great, the most vigorous could not express what I feel about those boys.'"

✦ ✦ ✦

FBI agents had been searching in the area to no avail until an informant known as Mr. X gave them an invaluable tip. It led them to a gravel road in rural Neshoba County, through a desolate area of red clay hills and scrub pines to an isolated farm. And so, it was early on the day of August 4 that FBI agents had ordered and supervised the excavation of a fairly recent earthen dam. Buried deep, deep in the ground, the bodies of the missing men were uncovered, stacked one on top of another.

✦ ✦ ✦

Early the next morning on August 5, the phone rang in Rhode Island. Our close family friend Elton Rayack was on the line. I heard Mom gasping.

Listening, she kept repeating at intervals, "Oh . . . Oh . . . Oh Eltie," in a low register.

When our friend Eltie, who was a professor of Luke's at the University of Rhode Island, had first opened the *New York Times* that morning, a main headline near the top of the front page dismayed him: "FBI Finds 3 Bodies Believed to Be Rights Workers." Just underneath, in the left column, the headline read: "GRAVES AT A DAM: Discovery Is Made in New Earth Mound in Mississippi."

By the time Eltie finished reading her parts of the article, Mom had slumped onto the floor of Dad's study, shivering and crying. Dad and I rushed over to hold her close. Dad pried the receiver from her hand, thanking Eltie for letting us know. Then he dressed as quickly as he could and drove to Babbie's, the general store at the top of the hill, to buy a copy of the *New York Times*.

Once she'd collected herself enough to stand, Mom hurried downstairs to the kitchen and switched on the radio.

Bubbe, frowning, hovered close by. The litany of her voice added a counterpoint to Mom's. Bubbe kept muttering in a mixture of English and Yiddish, "Oy . . . Oy . . . my Lushinka . . . Oy, those poor boys . . . *Oy veh ist mir.*"

I stood in the kitchen, my heart pounding, my jaw clenched. *How could anybody do this? Why are people so cruel?*

Chapter 13

GRIEF

In Meridian, helping the children cope with the devastating news was uppermost of Luke's concerns. He made this entry in his diary:

I went to the Community Center today and asked the kids *in the ancient Passover style* [emphasis added]:

"Why is this day different from all other days?"

The kids answered.

"Because Mickey and them are dead . . ."

"What were they like?" I asked, "I never had a chance to know them."

Many little arms were raised and all spoke at once. Answers like: "He had a beard . . . He used to play Frankenstein with us . . . He took us for drives in the country . . . He made us work hard . . . He talked about dignity."

"Why did he leave his home in New York to come to Meridian where life is so hard?"

"Because he knew that we needed him."

"He wanted to help us get our freedom."

"Freedom for what? What was Mickey really fighting for?"

The kids answered, "Freedom" and seemed puzzled.

Some said, "Civil Rights." Some said, "Equality."

Fran (age 14) said that Rita Schwerner, Mickey's wife, once said: "We want you to be able to live where you want and go where you want and love who you want."

I told them that perhaps the most important thing that Mickey was fighting for was love between all men.

I told them that Negroes can get a pretty good meal at Henderson's or Beals. They can survive without bowling or white movies. Mickey wasn't fighting for these things. [H]e was fighting for human dignity . . ."

I pointed to two Negro children who were buddies sitting together hand in hand.

"If [one of you was a white boy], you couldn't sit with your friend—you would never have a chance to know him, and this would be very sad for you, wouldn't it?"

They both nodded their heads and I am sure they understood. This is what Mickey was fighting for.

I asked them, "What would Mickey want you to do now? What can we do to carry on his work?"

Some of the kids said: "Fight for Freedom," but they seemed puzzled about what to do.

I said, "Learn about Freedom. What is the Civil Rights Bill?" They didn't seem to know.

Frank [one of the teenagers] . . . explained it to the kids:

"We went down to the Tasty Treat to test the Civil Rights Bill. They served some White Kids, but they wouldn't serve us. They called us n-----s and we went away."

I explained that Frank had goofed up. He should have filed a complaint against Tasty Treat.

The Civil Rights Bill is law and the Tasty Treat violated it.

The kids suggested that we should press the boycott against Woolworth's, Kress, and Newberry's. Mickey started it and our people are going there anyway. Let's tell them not to go.

✦ ✦ ✦

In the midst of their shock, the parents of Mickey, Andy, and James agreed that they wanted their sons to be buried side by side. Doing so would honor the cause for which they gave their lives and bear witness to their shared sense of brotherhood. Permission was not granted, however, because it violated Mississippi's strict segregation laws. Even in death Blacks and whites were kept apart in separate cemeteries. And so, with another insult adding injury to their grief, their parents arranged to have Mickey's and Andy's remains returned to the East Coast for burial.

As the shocking discovery of the bodies began to sink in, the Chaney family planned a private funeral for James. But for the wider civil rights community, this would not be enough. There was a compelling need for everyone to be able to come together in grief.

"What should we do?" Luke asked.

During the discussions, he first favored a march through Neshoba County where the murders had taken place but quickly reconsidered. He explained in a letter.

A march of civil rights workers and freedom school kids through Neshoba County to Philadelphia for the funeral was a powerful idea but the danger was too great.

[Instead] Gail and I felt that a silent walk of Negroes through the streets of Meridian would be a good thing. It would be a powerful expression of our concern for what happened and the common experience of grief, and the funeral procession would help to unify the Negro Community behind the Civil Rights movement.

We proposed this idea to Bob Gore, the leader of our project on Wednesday night and he agreed that we should do this.

Gail and I volunteered to be in charge of a committee to organize the funeral walk.

The next day, Thursday, August 6, Luke and Gail heard that the funeral would take place the following day. According to Luke, "We called the members of our committee together and went to work. The funeral was actually going to take place in the afternoon—a small quiet service for the Chaney family."

The committee planned a memorial service for the community to begin at seven o'clock in the evening at First Union Baptist Church. They mapped out routes for the funeral procession. "Negroes from the South side of town were to meet at Calvary Baptist Church at 6 o'clock; Negroes from the West side would meet at Mount Olive Baptist Church; and Negroes from East side and Red line would meet at New Hope and 31st Avenue Baptist Churches. Everyone would then walk from these churches to First Union." They checked city laws to make sure that none could be used to prevent them from walking and were relieved to find there were no laws pertaining to funeral processions.

The question of what they should bring proved a more divisive issue.

Someone suggested, "Let's carry a mock casket. That way we can prove this really is a funeral procession and not a demonstration."

But the Reverend Bill Hervey, who was white, objected to this. "I don't want people to focus their attention on the body. This has got to be about the life of James Chaney. And besides, passions are already running high. A casket might just inflame our people and lead to a riot. It's not a good idea."

"You're right, Reverend Bill, but—" Luke countered, "we can't whitewash the fact that a death has occurred. I don't give people credit for much imagination—especially when it comes to the subject of death. I feel strongly that the fact and horror of death must be deeply and shockingly understood."

Luke argued that stirring up people's emotions was necessary.

"People should have to look death in the face and be sick from it." He was hoping "this powerful mix of anger and indignation might lead them to work harder for the things Chaney died for." Perhaps looking death in the face would lead people to say, "never again."

Luke continued. "We've got to get them involved now while we can, they must learn from this, and they must swear to carry on the struggle for civil rights!"

Just then someone else entered the room and reported that the police had agreed to cooperate. Hearing this, the committee members decided not to carry a mock casket.

Freeman stepped forward and concluded, "The death of these boys tells the story of the Negro in America. The funeral will speak for itself."

Luke and Gail led the effort to organize the march, and there was no time to lose. In a letter, Luke captured the breathless momentum:

We only had time to notify the public on the day of the service [Friday, August 7] that the funeral would take place. We wanted to catch people before they left for work.

We called all the COFO staff and warned them that they would be awakened at 5 AM to distribute the leaflets.

We stayed up the whole night and mimeographed several thousand leaflets. I spent much of the night arranging who would go where.

At 5 AM, four carloads of COFO workers distributed the leaflets to different areas of Meridian.

I was sleepy as hell, but I was too busy to think about it—and it was nice to be up at dawn.

There were many other details that demanded attention. "Sue Brown, Gail, and I, and a group of lawyers and ministers met with the Chief of Police—Chief Gunn. He was very cooperative and offered us a police escort." Luke spoke up to remind him, "We don't want policemen with riot squad helmets in the church." Luckily Chief Gunn understood and agreed.

They also needed to notify the FBI.

We met with the FBI and told them the routes that we would follow. We selected good leaders among the COFO staff to lead the
walks from the various churches.

We prepared a radio announcement about the funeral. We
arranged for loudspeakers to carry the sermon to those outside the
church in case the church was filled.

In addition to his letter, Luke somehow found time to write in
his diary.

We are planning a great march. We shall dress in black and
march silently to the funeral of James Chaney. We hope that their
indignation will overcome their fear and that the Negro Community will unite for this event. We hope that this experience will be
a bond that ties them to the things that Chaney fought for. Many
of the Meridian Negroes have been frightened. We see the same
old faces at the mass meetings. The Negro Community must unite
in order to overcome. How tragic that men must die to bring this
about. How terribly important it is that men learn something from
this experience; the horror and brutality of this system, and the
desperate need for love and brotherhood in our times.

We hear about possible war in Vietnam. If you must blow our
world to pieces, wait at least until we have won our freedom.

✦ ✦ ✦

That evening, at six o'clock on August 7, the procession began with
marchers converging on the central church from four directions
like the corners of the Cross. Luke's route was from the south.

Reverend Culpepper and I led the Negroes from the South Side on
a walk from Calvary Baptist Church to First Union.

There weren't many people there at 6 o'clock when I arrived, and
this made me very angry.

Luke walked through the streets hollering to people on the sidelines.

March led by Luke and Reverend Culpepper through Meridian to James Chaney's memorial service. © 1976 George Ballis/Take Stock/TopFoto.

"We are going to a funeral for James Chaney. He died for us. Come and join us. Come and help us carry on his work!"

Luke described the somber and dignified march:

We began to walk. Reverend Culpepper has a great craggy face—a face, which tells a story of great suffering and great struggle. He is crippled and he walks with a grotesque stride, which brings his body high in the air and then low near the ground. He has struggled long and hard and it will take much more than a crippling disease to turn him back. He was proud to be leading his people through the streets of Meridian.

As we walked, more and more people joined our group. There were young people and old people.

It was particularly moving to see the old women—helping each other along, arm in arm, tottering along down Freedom's Road.

A police car moved slowly beside us with Negro policemen inside. They were determined to protect us, and it was comforting to have them there.

White people came out of their houses as we walked past. We were dressed in dark clothes and we walked silently and with great dignity. I feel certain that some of the white people must have felt sympathy and that some of them would even have joined us were they not afraid of the disapproval of their neighbors.

We reached the church without any incidents and there we met the Negroes who had walked from other parts of town. There were probably over 1,000 people gathered there in front of the First Union Baptist Church.

Having reached their destination, the emotionally laden service began.

The memorial service for James Chaney was an experience I will never forget. The service was a perfect blend of religious respect for the dead and a call to struggle for Freedom.

Bob Gore—the Negro project director of Meridian COFO and Bill Hervey, a white preacher from the National Council of Churches stood side by side at the pulpit, and they talked about Chaney.

Dave Dennis, assistant program director of the Mississippi Summer Project, gave the most impassioned speech I have ever heard. His voice was choked with emotion, and he cried with racking convulsive sobs. He was furious and felt that everyone in Meridian should have come to the funeral of James Chaney, and to those who didn't come, he said—

"I'm tired of going to funeral and memorial services. Too many of our best people killed—and you ought to be tired too. They tell me that I ought to love the white people who kill us, but I'm sick and tired of loving. I'm so full of anger now I can't love anymore—and you ought to be angry too. Everyone ought to fight the fight that they were fighting. To those who can sit back, who didn't come tonight, who won't carry on their fight, God damn your souls."

He cried and gasped, "I can't stand it anymore," and he left the pulpit.

Many people began to cry. The Chaney family began to cry and in this moment of grief, TV cameras moved in, bright lights were flashing, cameramen crowded around to catch the pain and sorrow on the faces of this family.

A man next to me cried loudly, and I felt tears streaming over my own face.

Reverend King, white chaplain of Tougaloo Southern Christian College, gave a very moving speech. He read letters from Mickey and Rita Schwerner. They told about the Community Center.

Rita wrote, "The Community Center is growing daily. Our library now has thousands of books. I go everywhere begging for paints and books and supplies. I no longer feel ashamed to beg. The need is so great." Rita talked about the conflict that she and Mickey felt. They wanted to stay and work and at the same time they wanted to start a family. "Things are so uncertain here. I wouldn't commit myself to the care of a puppy, let alone an infant." She said something about how they were going to begin work in the surrounding counties, "some of which are very dangerous. I wish that burned out station wagon could be shown to every person in America who has doubts."

This public reading of Rita's letters moved Luke and prompted him to reflect.

[I felt the utter] contrast between this crowded little Baptist Church and the Government of Mississippi. Rita and a Reverend had gone to the Governor's mansion [just after the disappearance]. Governor Johnson was talking with Governor Wallace of Alabama.

When Rita approached, Governor Johnson said, "I have no time for her." Guards drew bayonets and stepped in front of her as she pleaded for her husband.

The service concluded with singing, of course. "At the end of the evening, we all joined hands and sang with a great and beautiful feeling from the bottom of our hearts, 'We Shall Overcome.'"

At this moment, the songs were particularly filled with emotion at once poignant and fierce. "Mrs. Heidelberg and I walked out of the church arm in arm, and we sang again in the streets—'We Shall Overcome.'"

Afterward, as Gail and Luke were walking home, Ben Chaney, younger brother of James, came running up and called out, "Come with me Luke."

Luke wrote:

Ben is 12 years old and he looks very much like James. We walked hand in hand to Paines, and I bought him some ice cream. He talked about Mickey.

Mickey used to have a story hour and Ben loved it. The kids could pick out any book, and Mickey would read it. Ben said he misses the story hour.

Ben pleaded, "Luke, will you promise you'll have a story hour at the Community Center again?"

Without hesitation Luke replied, "Yes. I promise you, Ben."

Together they walked back to Ben's home.

Upon entering, Luke was nervous. Would the family feel he was intruding in this time of mourning? Luke was surprised.

Mrs. Chaney and some other people were sitting in the living room. They all greeted me when I walked in and it seemed strangely like any other day at the Chaney home.

I went back to the kitchen and had a few glasses of beer with some of the Chaney relatives. One guy told me about how he was too violent to join the movement.

Ben wanted to go out again for some food. We had to push the car to get it started, and we all went out to the Tasty Treat for some hamburgers and beer. There was a long banquet table and many of our COFO staff were there.

The camaraderie gave Luke pause.

It seems strange that after thinking so hard on death, we should so quickly become involved in the act of living—yet it was right.

We are living and loving and fighting hard for the things that Chaney lived for. We died a little with him, but we live a little for him.

Chapter 14

PERSISTENCE

Living up to the memory of James Chaney required resolute commitment, so Luke and Gail couldn't take the time to catch up on much-needed sleep. Since the beginning of the summer, Freedom School students from all around the state had been busily preparing for the culmination in their Freedom School Convention. It began early the very next morning after James Chaney's funeral, on Saturday, August 8.

As promised, it was a student-led affair. Early on, student leaders had decided to use the Meridian Freedom School as the location because of its large school building. According to Staughton Lynd, who was the Freedom School director: "Meridian possessed the palace of the Freedom School circuit, a three-story Baptist seminary which could easily house 100 delegates. Meridian young people, therefore, took on the complicated task of finding lodging and arranging transportation."

Andreesa's good friend Roscoe Jones was one of the two principal officers chosen statewide by their peers to lead the event. It was Roscoe who had first introduced Andreesa and her sisters to the Community Center shortly after it had opened. Through the summer, Roscoe had been spearheading the planning of the complicated logistics.

During daytime workshops, young leaders from around the state analyzed pressing problems they themselves had identified earlier in the summer. The issues included employment, housing, public accommodations, voter registration, education, and medical care. Each subcommittee came up with practical recommendations, which they drafted into resolutions and presented at the plenary session. In this way, the students created an actual political platform—a youth platform—for the Mississippi Freedom Democratic Party.

There was art too. The first evening, students from the Holly Springs Freedom School performed a play they had written themselves. And, of course, freedom songs were at the heart of the gathering. During lunchtimes, Roscoe Jones could be found at the center of the singing. All in all, it was a stunning student convention dedicated to building democracy.

Luke jotted into his diary: "Today (Saturday) at the Freedom School Convention, Staughton Lynd . . . told about Mickey, Chaney, and Andrew [and how] they went to investigate the burned church because it had been intended for a Freedom School."

Tragically, it was a Freedom School burned to the ground before it was born.

Luke continued: "Staughton said, 'When a soldier dies in battle, you pick up his gun and carry on his fight. When a soldier dies in a nonviolent battle, you pick up his dream and carry on his fight.'" Mississippi's teenage Black students at the convention were carrying on the dream of the three murdered men and the civil rights movement, gaining confidence and skills they'd need to lead the next generation. By all measures, their student convention was a resounding success.

✦ ✦ ✦

On Saturday, back at home, we hadn't heard from Luke yet, but we were reading the newspapers and tuning into the news on the television. Right after Eltie had called, Mom ordered our own subscription to the *New York Times*. Every morning, she now drove up to the top of the hill to collect our copy at the general store Babbie's. She sifted through the pile of newspapers set aside at the bay window that had handwritten names scrawled across the top.

An article in Saturday's *New York Times* described James Chaney's funeral and burial in Meridian. We had to flip to page seven to find it. We also saw segments of Dave Dennis's fiery, grief-stricken speech on TV and empathized with his outrage. Because of this, we understood the public view of James's funeral. But we didn't know how Luke felt, and we had no idea how involved he and Gail had been in planning the march and the community service.

In other news that day, a major story on the front page concerned the war in Vietnam. The headline read, "Resolution Wins." The events were ominous because the United States was being drawn more deeply into the conflict. Over the past week, two incidents had occurred that the Defense Department claimed were "deliberate attacks" on US naval destroyers in the Gulf of Tonkin off the coast of North Vietnam. On Friday, the day of James's funeral, Congress had responded to the provocation by passing a resolution granting President Johnson broad powers to conduct military operations in Vietnam without a formal declaration of war. Mom, Dad, and I talked about this news. We agreed it was very worrisome.

✦ ✦ ✦

Meridian Freedom School classes resumed on Monday, August 10, just after the student convention. Luke wrote about a play-acting session. He took on the role of a Black man attending a white church, while Ben Chaney played the part of the white preacher. Luke wrote that Ben was "plenty mean."

"Get out of here n----r," Ben said. "God is a white man."

Luke retorted, "No! We're all created in the image of God, so this God must be all colors. Black and white, yellow, and red too!"

Ben wouldn't listen. He kicked Luke out of his church, but Luke was satisfied.

"I must say, I gave him a pretty good fight."

✦ ✦ ✦

When Luke finally did call us at home, he explained how he and Gail had first thought about organizing a community memorial for James Chaney to take place as a march through Philadelphia, Mississippi. Just hearing him mention the word Philadelphia scared me stiff. I felt a rush of relief when he told me that they had quickly discarded that idea and had marched instead through Meridian. Luke was revved up from all the events of the past few days and talked quickly. He told us how emotional the march and the service had been, how Dave Dennis had spoken out passionately and bitterly so that he and everyone else broke down crying, and yet how all of it had occurred peacefully.

"Oh yeah," I interrupted him, "peacefully.... That's so good to hear, Luke."

Then he mentioned he'd soon be going to the site of the burntout Mt. Zion Church for a public memorial service to honor all three of the men murdered—James, Mickey, and Andy. Hearing this, I held my breath.

Mom, on the phone downstairs, asked softly, "Lucien, are you sure it will be safe?"

After we hung up, the word *peacefully* kept looping through my mind. The same question seemed to lurk after each time Luke called: *Are you safe?*

It was like a war zone. That, I realized, was a fitting analogy: a war zone within our own country. But for African Americans in the South, it was also a description of everyday life.

As my grandmother said succinctly, "*Oy veh.*"

✦ ✦ ✦

Luke and youthful Richard Henderson traveling from Meridian to the Mt. Zion
Memorial Service in Neshoba County. Photo by Donna Garde. Courtesy of Mark
Levy, Mark Levy Collection, Queens College/CUNY Rosenthal Library Archives.

The public memorial service to honor the three men took place
the next weekend, on August 16. About three hundred and fifty
people gathered. Among them were prominent representatives of
the national civil rights movement. Luke, Gail, and many of their
Freedom School students and other Meridian COFO workers and
community members traveled in cars and buses to the rural Mt.
Zion community, several miles from Philadelphia. For most of
them, it was the first time they had set foot in "bloody Neshoba

Mourners at Mt. Zion memorial service (Luke center). Photo by Mark Levy, Mark Levy Collection, Queens College/CUNY Rosenthal Library Archives.

County," the most infamous territory of all. As Luke had warned us, they stood solemnly before the charred ruins of the Mt. Zion Church.

Toward the end of the service Mrs. Fannie Lee Chaney spoke.

It's time for us to be close now, and if we're going to do something, we had better do it now. I want help. I want help and I need all of you all. . . .

Don't let those children's work go in vain. They dead. Don't let their work die. That's when freedom started. You all don't know, you all got parents, and they got lots of children that's gone. But none of them went like mine. It's hard. . . . It's hard.

But every time there's somethin' about freedom, I go. I got to go. . . . When the children come home this evenin' my head was hurtin'. They say, "Mama, you goin'?" I say, 'Yea, I'm goin'.' And I'm sure enough goin' even if nobody else don't go. I'm goin'. And here I am.

Chapter 15

MYSTERY UNTANGLED AND TRANSITION

At home, we were following the news about the murders, anxious to piece the story together and understand what had happened. Luke and his friends in Mississippi—and everyone connected personally in some way to the unfolding events of Freedom Summer—were closely monitoring the details. It was an urgent murder mystery.

Over time, the sequence of events emerged. The FBI code-named the case MIBURN for "Mississippi Burning." This is the story that the FBI ultimately put together.

On the fateful day of June 21, before they left Meridian, James, Mickey, and Andy had stopped to get haircuts from two brothers who were friends of James. It was an ordinary Sunday morning, it seemed, and a nice ritual to start off the day. James drove the COFO station wagon as they went to meet with members of the Mt. Zion community and inspect the burnt remains of the church. On the way back, Deputy Sheriff Cecil Ray Price passed them in his police cruiser by chance. Price recognized their station wagon and was tickled to see Mickey "Jew-boy" within his jurisdiction. Price had been hoping for just such an opportunity to catch him. Just inside Philadelphia city limits, Price stopped them and arrested James for speeding. It's alleged that Price told Mickey and Andy they'd be held as suspects in the church arson, as if that made any sense. He took them to the Neshoba County Jail where he kept them incommunicado for over six hours.

It was getting late and dark by the time the three young men were released. Civil rights workers were not supposed to drive after dark, but what else could they do? They set out with the intent to drive back to Meridian. Meanwhile, without their knowledge, Price alerted his fellow Klansmen. Price caught up with James, Mickey, and Andy near the county line. Close behind Price's police cruiser, an unmarked car followed, filled with Klansmen. Price flashed the lights of his cruiser, and James stepped on the gas, leading them on a high-speed chase before suddenly braking at the side of the road. Dragged from the station wagon, the three were forced into the backseat of the police car. Klansmen followed behind, now in two cars, one of which was their own COFO station wagon.

Heading back toward Philadelphia, the cars veered off before reaching town onto an unmarked dirt road.

When the cars stopped, one of the Klansmen yelled, "So, you wanted to come to Mississippi? Well, now we're gonna let you stay here."

Pulled from the car one by one, Mickey was shot in the heart and Andy too. James was the only one of the three who resisted.

Deputy Price drove back to Philadelphia to establish his alibi. The rest of the Klansmen loaded the bodies into the COFO station wagon and transported them to the remote location of Old Jolly Farm. There, a Klan member was waiting for them with a bulldozer. He was an excavator who worked for the owner of the land and had been hired to build a large earthen dam for a cattle pond. In raw red clay, deep into a hole fifteen feet down, the bodies were dropped one by one and covered up. Hidden under ten tons of dirt, the Klansmen were convinced it was forever.

When the FBI was unearthing the bodies on August 4, word got out to the local police. In retrospect, it is excruciating to know that Cecil Price, in his official role as deputy sheriff, escorted the bodies to the University of Mississippi Medical Center in the state capital of Jackson. A perfunctory autopsy was performed there. The death certificates read "cause of death unknown."

Resisting massive pressure from state and local authorities, James's mother, Fannie Lee Chaney, bravely gave permission for a second autopsy to be performed by an outside examiner. A doctor volunteering for Freedom Summer contacted a nationally known pathologist, David Spain, who flew in from the East Coast. Dr. Spain faced multiple hurdles and delays but, with dogged persistence, was finally able to reexamine James Chaney's body at the morgue. The doctors responsible for the first autopsy stood across from him. Dr. Spain's eyewitness account, published in *Ramparts Magazine*, was harrowing:

> I looked up at the three doctors opposite me. Their faces were stone . . . I could barely believe the destruction to these frail young bones. It was obvious to any first-year medical student that this boy had been beaten to a pulp. . . . I have been conducting examinations of this type for a quarter century, but for the first time I found myself so emotionally charged that it was difficult to retain my professional composure. I felt every fiber in my own body shaking, as I involuntarily imagined the scene at the time this youngster received such a vicious beating to shatter his bones in this incredible manner. . . . I felt like screaming at these impassive observers still silently standing across the table. But I knew that no rage of mine would tear their curtain of silence.

Three weeks after she'd granted permission for the second autopsy to be done, Mrs. Chaney's home was shot into and bombed. The bomb exploded, missing her home but damaging her neighbor's. Luckily, no one was hurt, but Mrs. Chaney had received a threat, and it wouldn't be the last.

✦ ✦ ✦

At home, we continued to follow the news, feeling a deep need to unravel the mystery of the murders. Simultaneously, we longed for closure. It was hard not to make conjectures about the future. I wondered, *Will there ever be a trial for the murderers in Mississippi? And if there is one, will they walk away scot-free? Because they always do.*

Just two days after James Chaney's funeral, the *New York Times* sent reporter John Herbers to cover the annual Neshoba County Fair. The fairgrounds were located within two miles of the now infamous earthen dam at Old Jolly Farm. As usual, white Mississippians from Meridian flocked to the fair. The eighty-six-year-old chairman of the fair, J. B. Hillman, explained to Herbers that "the people were determined not to let the scandal dampen the festivities."

Reading about this in Rhode Island, my stomach cramped, and my head involuntarily jerked to the side as if someone had slapped me hard. *How can people do this?* I thought. *They live so near each other, but there's a wall between them. For the whites, the murders are nothing, only a nuisance—like a fly needing to be swatted away.*

✦ ✦ ✦

At Andrew Goodman's service in New York City, his father delivered an eloquent eulogy, drawing on values laid forth by President Lincoln in his Gettysburg Address and in the Declaration of Independence.

> Our grief, though personal, belongs to our nation. This tragedy is not private. It is part of the public conscience of our country.
>
> It is necessary, especially in such a time of agony, to confront ourselves with our own history and the social sickness that still remains long after "the binding together of our nation's wounds" that was our Civil War. . . .

Throughout our history, countless Americans have died in the continuing struggle for equality. We shall continue to work for this goal, and we fervently hope that Americans so engaged will be aided and protected in this noble mission.

For ourselves, we wish to express our pride in our son's commitment and that of his companions now dead; and that of his companions now alive, now in Mississippi, acting each hour to express those truths that are self-evident.

✦ ✦ ✦

All around the state of Mississippi, civil rights activists were carrying on, continuing the work of Freedom Summer. In Meridian, the Community Center that Mickey had started was alive and well, echoing with the voices and activities of staff members, volunteers, local adults, and the children. The Community Center served as an oasis welcoming everyone, most especially the children who claimed it as a second home. Like Luke, most of the volunteers had never had the chance to meet Andy, Mickey, or James, but nevertheless, these activists were following in their footsteps, inspired by their self-sacrificing dedication to the cause of freedom. As Andy's parents hoped, they too were striving to "shine a beacon of light."

The volunteers were making a difference in the local community and certainly in the lives of the children and their Freedom School students. The experience was also adding meaning, of course, to their own lives. Everyone involved was transformed because of this brave experiment. But would it make a difference in the long run? Would their work actually contribute to social change? Perhaps the Democratic National Convention, on the horizon, would provide a place for them to find out.

✦ ✦ ✦

A time of transition now approached as Luke and Gail would soon be leaving Mississippi and traveling, along with others, to the convention in Atlantic City, New Jersey. Sixty-eight delegates representing the Mississippi Freedom Democratic Party—sixty-four Blacks and four whites—would travel east by bus. Meanwhile, Freeman had decided to stay behind to continue working with the children. He planned to stay on in Meridian through the fall and winter.

As Luke got ready to leave Meridian, he found time to reflect.

This is my last week in Mississippi and it is hard for me to leave.

. . . It is tragic that barriers so foolish as color differences prevent whites and Negroes from knowing and loving each other—and it is only when these barriers are destroyed that any of us can find freedom.

I wonder, what will become of the project we began?

Will Roscoe [Jones] be accepted to the "white" Meridian high school?

Will we get served at Weidman's [restaurant]?

Will Andreesa become a doctor? Will Ed become an atomic physicist—or will they become a maid and a janitor because they were born with skin that is black . . . ?

What will become of Lilly? How long can she sing and dance in a world so cruel and tough? And what about Lance and Lenray and Larry and little Rose Mary with the mischievous and adorable upper lip?

The Community Center with its green sagging bench, lavender room, bookcases, crank calls, and a pile of kids with Freeman at the bottom—and Sam Brown who changed his name to Freedom with his three gold teeth embellished by stars?

✦ ✦ ✦

When the day of departure arrived, Luke was a passenger in the car. Gazing out the window as they drove away, he was filled with emotion.

"Mississippi was hell but I was very happy there. The sky was bright with stars, there was sunshine and sunflowers, and I was happy in my work."

On the drive east to Atlantic City, he observed the changing landscape. Memories surfaced of carefree summers when he'd hitchhiked on his own across the country back and forth to Mexico. There was so much for him to absorb and process during this brief interlude.

Luke was also anticipating the days ahead at the Democratic National Convention with a sense of combined promise and anxiety.

Chapter 16

MISSISSIPPI FREEDOM DEMOCRATIC PARTY ON THE NATIONAL STAGE

The delegates of the Mississippi Freedom Democratic Party (MFDP) arrived in Atlantic City determined to claim seats at the national convention. Their mission was to challenge the Mississippi "regulars" that were selected by a party whose motto could well have been "whites only need apply." The seating dispute would be taken up by the Credentials Committee. Many members of the committee were identified as sympathetic to the cause of civil rights. To help secure the needed votes, Luke and other summer volunteers planned to spend hours inside lobbying for the cause.

Outside on the boardwalk, civil rights workers set up a vigil. Many held handmade signs. Luke's adapted a line from a Bob Dylan song: "It's blowing in the wind—Freedom." They also confronted onlookers with a gruesome truth, having towed the burnt-out shell of a COFO station wagon driven on a fateful night by three young men. As Luke had argued in Meridian when they were planning the march to James Chaney's funeral, "Don't let people look away from death."

Vigil at night on the boardwalk at the National Democratic Convention.
© 1976 George Ballis/Take Stock/TopFoto

MFDP delegates and supporters staged a sit-in demonstration on the
boardwalk that continued day and night throughout the convention.

Luke and his fellow activists were hopeful. SNCC Chairman John Lewis wrote in his moving memoir, *Walking with the Wind* (1998):

> How could we not prevail? The law was on our side. Justice was on our side. The sentiments of the entire nation were with us. I couldn't see how those convention seats could be kept from us.
>
> That's how everyone felt. The sense of elation and excitement among the MFDP contingent . . . was palpable.

But against this backdrop, President Johnson was busy preparing for his nomination. His goal was to maintain a scripted, well-controlled Democratic convention. He had stepped in as president, under great duress, when President Kennedy was assassinated. Johnson knew he would be nominated—it was a foregone conclusion, but in early July, he had signed the Civil Rights Act of 1964. He feared a white backlash.

On Saturday, before the convention began, TV cameras rolled in the hearing room. Fannie Lou Hamer, a little-known MFDP delegate, rose to speak to the Credentials Committee. Formerly a sharecropper, she was now the party's vice-chair. Seated by her side was Rita Schwerner, Mickey's wife, whose quiet presence reminded everyone of the high stakes involved. Mrs. Hamer described brutal experiences she'd endured when she had tried to register to vote in Mississippi. "If the Freedom Democratic Party is not seated now, I question America. Is this America, the land of the free and the home of the brave, where we have to sleep with our telephones off the hooks because our lives be threatened daily because we want to live as decent human beings, in America?" Upset, President Johnson decided to hold an impromptu news conference on TV, interrupting coverage of her testimony. Johnson wanted to distract the nation, but his ploy proved unsuccessful. That evening, all TV news stations broadcast excerpts of Fannie Lou Hamer's powerful speech.

✦ ✦ ✦

In Rhode Island, watching TV in Bubbe's cozy bedroom off the kitchen, my parents, Bubbe, and I were completely mesmerized by her speech. We were also transfixed by any views we could see of the vigil on the boardwalk. We didn't want to miss a moment of news about the convention. We analyzed details and constantly chattered over each other.

"Did you see that?" blurted Dad, squinting at a sign at the vigil.

"*Unh*?!" Bubbe exclaimed, wildly waving her arm, and pointing at the screen. "*Iz dat Lushinka*? Maybe?" Her waving grew wilder and her voice more commanding, "*I t'ink zo! Over d'ere!*"

"Oh Bubbe, did you really see him?" I asked unbelievingly because all I could see was a general mass of weaving bodies almost indistinguishable from one another. "I don't!"

Then the picture switched to another scene.

Mom uttered, "Shh! Pay attention. They're going to play some of Fannie Lou Hamer's speech again."

Dad glanced over at Mom approvingly. "Fannie Lou. She's really something!"

"What's happening behind closed doors, do you think?" Mom asked. "What don't we know?"

And where is Luke in all of this? I wondered.

✦ ✦ ✦

Meanwhile in Atlantic City, Luke was busy with the vigil and lobbying the Rhode Island state delegation. He approached individuals and met the group, trying to convince them to support the MFDP.

In a letter to Free, he lamented, "Our Rhode Island delegates are impossibly ignorant! . . . [I]t was painful to hear them talk in political terms about a problem we know to be such a human problem."

Wasn't it obvious which delegation deserved to be seated? Luke's frustration was widely shared. The civil rights activists now faced a quandary—the stark demarcation between protests and politics. Protests are based on morality. Politics are based on compromise and power. It was a rude awakening.

Chaotic meetings and proposals filled the next several days. Out in the open, Johnson's emissaries pushed a compromise to resolve the seating dispute. Surreptitiously, behind the scenes, they used strongarm tactics. The Mississippi challengers never suspected they were being spied upon. But their phones were tapped by the FBI, acting on President Johnson's orders. Threats made to individual Credentials Committee members chipped away support for the MFDP.

Unaware of these back-door manipulations, supporters of the civil rights movement continued to hold their vigil and lobby members of Congress. Luke not only met Rhode Island delegates but also assisted those lobbying Wyoming and Montana. He wrote a letter to Rhode Island Senator Claiborne Pell and appealed to Pell in person.

"Senator Pell is on our side," Luke noted with relief in his letter to Free, "and that's encouraging."

✦ ✦ ✦

Luke's interaction with Senator Pell may have been meaningful to him because he had campaigned as a volunteer when Pell first ran for the Senate in 1960. I recall stacks of brochures Luke lugged home as he prepared to canvass voters door-to-door.

"Voting's a big part of what it means to be a citizen," he had explained to me.

That was the first election in which Luke was able to vote. For me, at age thirteen, it marked a political awakening. For the first time, I paid attention to who was voting for whom and why. Kennedy or Nixon? As usual in our neighborhood, my family stood apart, outnumbered, this time for being registered Democrats.

✦ ✦ ✦

In Atlantic City, the Democratic convention would officially begin on Tuesday evening. Thus, it was the "day of decision" when the "Mississippi question" needed to be resolved, either by compromise in the Credentials Committee or in a wider floor fight.

"The Atlantic City Compromise," proposed with President Johnson's blessing, consisted of three parts:

1. Two MFDP representatives would be seated as at-large delegates but *not* within the Mississippi delegation.
2. Members of the regular Mississippi delegation would be required to sign a loyalty oath, promising to support the Democratic party's nominees for president and vice president in the general election.
3. Regarding all *future* conventions, the national Democratic party pledged to bar racial discrimination in state delegations.

While the challengers were debating whether to accept the compromise, an announcement on TV interrupted the feed, stating that the Credentials Committee had just "unanimously approved" it. This caused them great consternation. Had they lost every supporter they'd counted on including their own lawyer? Later, they would learn that the vote was not unanimous, but it did pass out of committee. The outcome was predictable. That evening the compromise would pass by voice vote on the convention floor.

Of course, it was not a *real* compromise, foisted as it was on the challengers. Would they accept its terms? No! They rejected it unanimously. Mrs. Hamer famously remarked, "We didn't come all this way for no two seats."

Most Mississippi "regulars" refused to sign the loyalty oath and departed. Unsurprisingly, most of them would go on to support the

GOP candidate, Barry Goldwater, in the general election. White backlash. They defected just as Johnson had feared and as Dad had predicted before Luke even left for Mississippi.

That evening, as the convention began, twenty-two sympathetic delegates from other states gave their own passes to the challengers. The MFDP staged a sit-in. They took to the floor and dramatically sat down on seats left vacant in the Mississippi section. Luke observed all of this from inside Convention Hall. Members of the press had handed out passes so activists could enter the hall. Luke wrote to Free: "We got tickets and sat in the ABC Press Box on the night the Mississippi regulars walked out, and the Freedom delegates moved in to take their places. It was very exciting to see this."

The challengers didn't sit for long, however, before security guards hustled them out. Nevertheless, they'd sat defiant before a national audience.

Many civil rights activists worried, *Had Freedom Summer failed in its goal?* Being unable to achieve their central mission—to be seated at the Democratic convention—proved to be a crushing blow. In Mississippi, they had worked doggedly against brutal odds and had played by all the rules. They had come well prepared to make their case to the American people. What they asked for was clear—essential ingredients of freedom in a democratic society: respect, equality, and the right to vote.

Having failed, the challengers and most of their supporters left Atlantic City disheartened. They felt betrayed by liberal white politicians, whom they had erroneously viewed as partners. Black brothers and sisters in the movement carried a lingering, bitter taste with them. They would never again naively entrust their hopes to the whims of white politicians.

Luke held onto his optimism, writing to Free that at least "the ruling barring discrimination in the future was a real victory." Having participated for the first time in national politics may have contributed to his upbeat mood.

Protest by Mississippi Freedom Democratic Party (MFDP) on the boardwalk, August 10, 1964. © 1976 George Ballis/Take Stock/TopFoto.

✦ ✦ ✦

At home, watching the convention on TV, my parents, Bubbe, and I were not attuned to the grave disappointment most of the challengers experienced. We kept watching the convention proceedings with great interest. We felt the power of the challengers' sit-in, the civil rights vigil on the boardwalk, and most especially Fanny Lou Hamer's unforgettable speech. We talked about the new ruling that would bar any state from discriminating in how delegates were chosen for all future Democratic National Conventions. This part of the "compromise" seemed to promise more fairness and positive possibilities for Black-white integration. We were ignorant of the stakes involved and the betrayal felt by most activists.

✦ ✦ ✦

Failure of the MFDP delegates to be seated was a significant blow to the civil rights movement as a whole. Historian John Dittmer has captured the poignancy and distress of this moment in his book *Local People: The Struggle for Civil Rights in Mississippi* (1994). He quoted Joyce Ladner, a SNCC activist, saying, "For many people Atlantic City was the end of innocence."

John Lewis agreed in his memoir.

It was power politics that did in the MFDP, politics at its worst, really.

. . . That crisis of confidence, the spirit of cynicism and suspicion and mistrust that infects the attitude of many Americans toward their government today, began, I firmly believe, that week in Atlantic City.

It was a major letdown for hundreds and thousands of civil rights workers, both black and white, young and old people alike who had given everything they had to prove that you could work through the system.

They felt cheated.

They felt robbed.

It sent a lot of them outside the system.

These activists were exhausted and needed time to recoup. Many scholars have described it as "battle fatigue," akin to the shock experienced by soldiers returning home from war. And it was like that—it was the Civil War that had never truly ended.

Part Three

TRANSITION
AND RETURN

Chapter 17

RESPITE AND NEW BEGINNINGS

Leaving the Democratic convention, the time arrived at last for Luke to come home. Gail joined him on the journey north. Once again, at home, we anticipated his arrival, overflowing with excitement but also, this time, with a sense of relief. I accompanied Dad when he picked them up in Kingston at the quaint old train station, just past the University of Rhode Island. Hearing the train whistle, I jumped up and down, pumping my arms like a little kid. Luke grinned as he disembarked, lugging his small suitcase. Right behind him Gail was beaming.

She's so pretty, I thought, *and now he's here!* But I was taken aback. *Boy, does he ever look tired. Oh, my brother . . .*

Their days at home were filled with conversations around the kitchen table—our getting to know Gail, hearing their stories, and learning to sing freedom songs. There seemed to be a constant parade of newspaper reporters and photographers coming and going. Several articles appeared in the *Providence Journal* and the *Evening Bulletin* with interviews and photographs of Luke and Gail. To me, it felt like a hero's welcome.

Luke and Gail hiked across the Jamestown Bridge to Newport and talked about Mississippi. He took time to write to Free.

I am home in Rhode Island and already I am homesick for Mississippi. I really hated to leave you and the Grahams and Mr. Figgers,
and the kids. How good it was that we bumped into each other on
that airplane. That was the beginning of the most meaningful days
of my life. . . . I was scared out of my mind in those days in Memphis—death seemed imminent and I didn't realize that life richer
than I had ever known it was awaiting us in Meridian. . . . You are
a good and important friend to me Free and I think that you are
doing a powerful good job with the kids. I'm glad that you are staying—the kids really need you. . . . I miss you and wish I could be
with you in Meridian.

Your good friend,
Luke

✦ ✦ ✦

In our time together, I loved the countless songs Luke taught me in
his twangy, gutsy voice. Many of the freedom songs derived from
old gospel tunes that had been sung for years in Black churches—
songs like "Woke Up This Morning." We blared out the words,
substituting "my mind stayed on freedom" for the original hymn's
lyrics of "my mind stayed on Jesus." Reverend Wesby wrote the
freedom verses when he was in jail in Mississippi, arrested for
the "crime" of being a Freedom Rider protesting segregation on
interstate buses.

The origin of different freedom songs was eclectic. "They Say
That Freedom Is a Constant Struggle" may have been composed
earlier in the summer by SNCC member Sam Block after the disappearance of Chaney, Schwerner, and Goodman. Its slow, plain-
tive melody evokes the mixed emotions of grief and continuing
struggle. Next, Luke lovingly sang a song that asked: Who am I?
What do I want? What will I fight for? Some songs, like "We Shall
Overcome," grew out of composed hymns, and others were based
on folksongs. With gusto, we belted out "Ain't gonna let nobody

turn me around / . . . gonna keep on a-walkin', keep on a-talkin' / Marchin' down to freedom's land." The original spiritual this song was based on was about "keepin' on to Calvary."

Luke, Gail, and I sang these songs and ever so many more. It was hard for us to stop singing even to eat. The songs gave back energy by feeding the soul. To complement our singing with physical sustenance, Bubbe made sure there was plenty of food to go around. Altogether, their visit left us feeling full, but when they left, I was wishing for more.

✦ ✦ ✦

Having graduated a year early from high school, I spent the next week packing for college and preparing to leave home. Before returning to his studies at Stanford Medical School, Luke accompanied Gail to meet her family in Pittsburgh. He enjoyed getting to know her nine-year-old sister. As he would with any child, he asked for her opinions on any topics they discussed and took her answers seriously. She was impressed.

Soon afterward, I said goodbye to Mom and Bubbe. They stood together in the driveway, waving as Dad drove me off to freshman orientation at the University of Rochester in Upstate New York. I had never seen the campus before and thought the quad was beautiful, graced with stately, tall Dutch elm trees. I was quickly swept up in my new milieu.

Meanwhile, Luke said goodbye to Gail and flew off to the West Coast.

✦ ✦ ✦

None of us in the North knew that down in Meridian on the night of August 31, Free was awakened at 1:30 a.m. by the whizz of a gunshot and window glass shattering nearby. The bullet flew just above where he lay and lodged in the far wall. Terrified, he

Freeman resting during the summer in the room he and Luke shared. Photo from Luke's scrapbook. Courtesy of Syrtiller Kabat.

Gail wrote in a speech: "I lived with a wonderful couple, Sarah and Timothy Graham and their daughter Edna up on 46th Avenue. Two other civil rights workers [Luke and Freeman] lived next door with Mrs. Graham's father. One night the father's house was shot into, narrowly missing Freeman . . . who slept under the window that faced the street. But the Grahams just patched up the window and continued to make us feel as welcome as if nothing had happened."

managed to slip to the floor and hide under his bed. According to a CORE "Personnel Report":

> An attempt was also made on Freeman's life. . . . The local FBI and the local Police informed our office that they had reliable information that the shot was meant to kill him and not just to scare him.

They advised us to have him either leave the state or to transfer to another project. After meeting with the Jackson Staff, it was decided that he should take a vacation . . . for two weeks and then return to Meridian.

HE PLANS TO STAY FOR A YEAR.

In their next phone call, Free told Luke what had happened. Of course, he admitted he was frightened but still seemed to take it in stride, determined as he was to continue in the fight for freedom.

✦ ✦ ✦

Not long after Luke had left Pittsburgh, Gail requested a leave of absence from her studies at Radcliffe College. She, too, wanted to go back to Meridian to continue her work. In a letter she sent to the college administrators and to her friends, she explained:

[Before we came, many Negro people] were satisfied with a goal of "separate but equal" because they knew no whites [for whom] they would like to have the freedom to know. But in the community center, as we talked together and sang songs and ate lunch together and "monkeyed" with the kids, in the . . . homes where we helped wash dishes or ate watermelon or sat in the living room talking with "our" families we gradually came to be trusted and loved, not as white people but as people.

If all the white volunteers went home to their nice homes and good schools, leaving the families we stayed with [and] the children we taught, to bear the brunt of Mississippi's attempt to force closed the crack we made in "the closed society," I doubt if the new trust and understanding would endure.

Luke approved of Gail's decision and probably envied her choice to return. He missed his friends in Mississippi, the intensity of their community life, and the great sense of purpose they shared. The transition back to medical school was not easy for him.

Gail Falk. Courtesy of Syrtiller Kabat.

Meridian served as his touchstone. Letters began arriving, often with photos included. They reminded him of the continuing need and possibilities for protest, teaching, and action.

✦ ✦ ✦

In Rochester, beginning college, I dedicated myself to my studies. My favorite class was an overview of Western civilization. By the end of the first week, our professor, Hayden White, asked us to hand in a paper comparing Sigmund Freud's *Civilization and Its Discontents* (1930) with Karl Marx's *The Communist Manifesto* (1848). I'd never read these slim treatises, but I was familiar with the authors. Mom believed in Freud. She'd spent five years of my early childhood undergoing psychoanalysis. Dad championed the oppressed and took to heart Marx's maxim. "From each according to his ability, to each according to his need." There were family stories about how Dad had courted Mom in Chicago. While they huddled together on a city park bench, he read her passages from Marx's *Das Capital* (1867). That didn't sound so romantic to me, but what did I know? It worked.

Presto! Just like that, I was steeped in an intellectual world that reminded me of conversations Luke and I had when we sat around the kitchen table. As a premed student, I had science to study too.

During this time, Luke and I had a phone call. He sounded a bit downcast.

"I just wish I were in Meridian. So much is going on there. It's hard to stay away."

I understood and was sad to hear he was discontented.

"But I'll get back there as soon as I can," he hastened to add.

We talked about Johnson and Goldwater and the upcoming presidential election before saying goodbye.

✦ ✦ ✦

Soon after my phone call with Luke, I passed a student while crossing the quad on my way to the library. Noticing the novel I was carrying, he struck up a conversation. A week or two later, a coed from down the hall knocked on the door of my dorm room, announcing that I had a phone call. This was a first.

"Would you like to meet me for a cup of coffee?" he asked.

"Yes," I answered shyly.

At the café, we talked about ideas and books.

"Eureka!" I blurted out later as I raced down the hall of the dorm, my heart beating fast. "This is what I've been waiting for!"

None of the other boys I'd met had engaged me in conversations about ideas. And who did this remind me of?

Chapter 18

RETURN TO MERIDIAN

At the earliest opportunity, in mid-November, Luke returned to Meridian for six weeks. Stanford Medical School agreed he could substitute work in Mississippi as an elective for one of his clinical rotations. Of course, his diary went along too.

> I am happy to be back in Meridian. I arrived in the night and slept on the floor of the COFO office under the ping pong table. There were many cockroaches and a good number of them crawled over me.
> ... [Now] I'm living with a brave old woman, Mrs. J.

Luke and the children eagerly reconnected. He was struck anew by their resilience and by the camaraderie they shared. "I went out for dinner with some of the kids. We had chitterlings (called chitlins—pig's intestines)—and they smelled something terrible. If they can eat chitlins, they can overcome almost anything."

Soon, Luke fell into a routine and so did the children. Each day after school, young Patty of the Thompson sisters would arrive at the Community Center where Judy Wright was helping to staff the COFO office.

Before long, she'd look up and ask, "Is he here yet?"

Judy knew exactly who she meant.

Luke with Lance Williams (5th Street Red), sisters Andreesa and Dorothy
Thompson, and Linda Martin in front of the new COFO office, where they
moved in the fall of 1964. Photo by Bill Rodd. Used by permission of Thomas
Whitney Rodd.

Judy and her husband, Frank, had come to Meridian in October.
She explained why they came in her memoir, *Acts of Resistance: A
Freedom Rider Looks Back on the Civil Rights Movement* (2019):
"After the murders of the three young men, we had been sent to
fill in the shocked and heartbroken gap left in the COFO staff.
They needed more people to work on voter registration, the Free-
dom School that had been set up that summer, the picketing of

segregated restaurants and hotels, and all the other efforts aimed at ending segregation and the ongoing brutality and humiliation targeting blacks." Judy was mostly working in the COFO office, while Frank was teaching at the Freedom School.

Judy had deep experiences in the civil rights movement, having been a Freedom Rider in 1961. She had ridden an integrated inter-state bus into Mississippi and as a result, as she'd expected, spent six weeks locked up in the notorious Parchman State Prison. True to its reputation, her experience had been harrowing.

Now working at the COFO office in Meridian, Judy looked forward each afternoon to the arrival of the children—Patty, Lance, and Lenray. She wrote:

> Most days in Meridian, I'd be planning a demonstration or checking out finances at my desk in the COFO office at about three o'clock when school got out. It wouldn't be long before my little ten-year-old friend Patty Thompson would come flouncing in the door, usually followed closely by Lenray and Lance. . . . The three kids pranced around the long thin room. . . . But it was really only a polite delay before what they really wanted came right out. "Where's Luke? Is he here? Is he here?" . . . When the COFO door would swing open and Luke, dressed in his usual dark jeans and a plaid shirt would arrive . . . [they] would drop what they were doing and rush over to him, trying to get hold of whatever part of his body they could capture . . . a hand, a shoulder, even a finger. Then they would all be enclosed and wrapped in his affection. None were left out.

✦ ✦ ✦

Apart from playing with the children, there was much else for Luke to do. In hopes of finding "friends of civil rights," Luke and Gail reached out to the white community. Luke wrote: "We had intended to go to a Synagogue tonight. . . . Jews should understand better than most the horrors of prejudice. But the rabbi here said, 'We have suffered for 2,000 years. Let them suffer.'"

Undeterred, Gail and Luke showed up on another evening for Shabbos service, wearing freedom pins to make sure they'd be easily identified. Gail reported: "Received courteously, but definitely coolly. Keep in mind that we had . . . become accustomed to the invariably warm, effusive welcome we received at every single black congregation (and there were many!). . . . No one at Temple Israel suggested that we come back."

✦ ✦ ✦

Since the segregated public school was now in session, classes at Freedom School started late in the afternoon. Although many students were committed to sports, other activities, and chores, and thus too busy to attend, a stalwart core of students continued to show up eager to read and talk.

One afternoon, fifteen-year-old Bettye Manual created quite a stir when she arrived with her hair cropped short, sporting a natural cut. Afros were just beginning to be seen on TV and in magazines, but no teenage girls in Meridian had dared to try the new look. In one of her letters, Gail wrote that Bettye explained to her peers: "I feel that straightening hair is a sign of the Negro being ashamed. It shows that the Negro thinks the white man's standard of beauty is the only way to judge beauty. I want to show people that I'm not ashamed of my hair texture." A lively discussion ensued.

It felt cozy on cold nights when the small group huddled together near a gas stove. Luke brought his stethoscope to biology class so they could listen to their heart sounds. He wrote: "Frank, a Freedom School teacher, listens every day and says, 'Well, I made it through another day.' Some couldn't hear anything and were afraid that they might not have a heart."

Gail Falk teaching Freedom School students in the fall of 1964. Courtesy of
Gail Falk.

Luke also assisted Gail in her freedom class, challenging the
students to consider questions about segregation, the new civil
rights laws, school rules, and social norms. He jotted into his diary:
"we discussed a poem by Langston Hughes." *What happens to a
dream deferred?* "We felt that our dream of freedom had been
deferred and . . . it was time to act and make it a reality."

In her letters, Gail suggested that, by November, student atten-
dance was "flagging . . . we needed to do something more active
and concrete with the teenagers." At a meeting, the volunteers
and staff discussed how best to develop young leadership. They
decided to begin a program of testing the Civil Rights Act. Unlike

the summer, civil rights workers were no longer prohibited from participating in sit-ins or other actions. This opened up a whole new avenue for taking action, and they were gung-ho to do so.

The Civil Rights Act of 1964 had been signed into law by President Johnson on July 2, the day Luke left Rhode Island for his Freedom Summer orientation. The law banned segregation in public places, including restaurants, parks, and hotels. But getting businesses to comply was another matter in Mississippi. If only the law was like a magic wand, so you could just wave it and make segregation disappear—*poof!* But in the real world, going out to test the law was necessary. Gail explained:

> Our strategy was for two white COFO workers to go to the restaurant and order something to confirm that we could be served and that it wasn't a private club. We also scouted out each restaurant for signs that it was engaged in interstate commerce.
>
> . . . In some cases, we went to talk to the restaurant owners in hopes that they would agree to desegregate voluntarily.
>
> Every day after Freedom School we went and tested three or four places.

Luke described how they prepared:

> Gail read the Civil Rights Bill to her Freedom Class and we discussed ways of testing the law in Meridian. Kids talked of places they wanted to test . . . the Bowling Alley. None of the kids has ever bowled and the idea of this "forbidden fruit" has a magical quality. The Skating Rink, the White Teen Center with its ping pong tables and juke boxes. . . . Wideman's Restaurant, a swanky place where you have to dress up to go.

The teens learned how to fill out affidavits for cases in which they weren't served. Another COFO worker, Eric Weinberger, led workshops on nonviolence in order to role-play various situations they might encounter. Luke noted, "So, in Freedom Class we planned, [and as we] worked for freedom, we came to understand better what we were fighting against and what we were fighting for."

Out in the community:

Sometimes . . . we were served grudgingly, and the waitress would slam the food on the counter.

Sometimes kindly and there was "Come back again." I went with 5 brave young high school girls to Woolworths, Kress, and Newberry's. Bettye Manual was spokesman for the group. . . . They were sick of drinking coca cola after integrating the three restaurants, but they were mighty happy.

Sometimes maliciously . . . at Chick-n-Treat, they gave us hamburgers with hot pepper sprinkled liberally on top. I howled and my mouth is still burning. The Bastards. Sometimes it's hard to be nonviolent.

But mostly we were turned away and insulted and spit upon and pushed—and at the Toddle House there was a mob.

✦ ✦ ✦

The night before Thanksgiving was a prelude to events that would take a more challenging turn. That evening, Luke and Gail went out testing with teenagers at the Tudor and Sims Drugstore. Following protocol, Luke and Gail entered first. They sat down at the counter and were served quickly. The waitress, who had no idea who they were, told them, when they inquired, that the counter would be open for another full hour. However, when the teens approached, she refused to serve them. Afterward, one of the teen leaders, Willie Clark, filled out an affidavit:

We walked over to the soda fountain and asked to be served two cokes and two grape pops. The waitress walked [away] . . . and said something to the manager. . . . When the manager came over, he said the fountain was closed.... [I] asked could we get the drinks to go. He said no. He said the place was closed. I asked what time the place usually closed. He said 7:00. I asked him to give his name. He replied, "You know me, I'm the big man"... and continued, "Now get them out of here." We politely walked out.

✦ ✦ ✦

The next day, November 26, was Thanksgiving. I was back home in Rhode Island for the holiday. I had taken the train the day before, and my boyfriend, Al Schwartz, came along with me. Dad picked us up at the station in Kingston. Mom was waiting eagerly by the kitchen door. She warmed to Al immediately, before I even had the chance to introduce him, as soon as she saw us entering the back porch holding hands.

It was my first visit home since I had left for college. My sister, Alix, was also back for the holiday. She had flown in from California with her new boyfriend, Gregory. Early Thanksgiving morning, Alix and I collected bittersweet in the woods, a familiar ritual we had always enjoyed together. We draped the orange-red bittersweet around the dining room. We helped Mom decorate the table with a festive tablecloth and a colorful clay candelabra that Luke had brought home as a gift from Mexico. So, we were a cozy group gathered around the table on Thanksgiving afternoon, chattering between bites. We didn't hear from Luke and hadn't expected him to call that day.

We knew he was busy. But how busy? We had no idea.

Chapter 19

JAIL

On Thanksgiving Day, taking advantage of the school holiday, Gail, Judy Wright, and six high school students went out testing in the morning. Gail was the driver. Their first stop was the A&W Root Beer stand where students had previously been refused service. As they left, one of the waitresses followed them out and wrote down their license plate number.

Gail asked her with disdain, "Do you want our registration number too?"

The waitress didn't answer.

Their next stop was down the street at the Tudor and Sims Drugstore, the focus of the affidavit Willie had filled out the night before. This morning, however, the manager, Mr. Tudor, did not even do them the courtesy of making an excuse.

He simply roared, "Get out of here!" and followed the students outside.

The police, who he must have called, drove up, and the officer went over to talk to Mr. Tudor just as they left. The cop followed and soon beeped for Gail to pull over. He approached as she was rolling down the window.

"Well, why don't you take 'em downtown where they belong?" he asked with a sneer. "Don't be bringin' 'em out here where they're not wanted."

Gail had no intention of taking his advice. So, she headed across town to the Whirly-Dip, which sold soft-serve ice cream. The policeman followed again and beeped when she turned into the driveway.

This time, pointing emphatically, he shouted, "Drive straight down to the police station!"

"What for?" she asked.

"You made an improper turn."

At the police station, Willie Clark started to get out of the car.

The cop yelled, "You! Get back in the car. I want to talk to her, alone."

In the station, he announced that her bond would be twenty-nine dollars.

"Is this what you usually charge?" she inquired.

"No," he replied curtly. "But it's what the sergeant told me to charge you."

By chance, Gail happened to have enough cash in her pocket to cover the cost. Her court date was set for Saturday, two days away.

Departing the police station, Gail doggedly proceeded back to the Whirly-Dip. On the way, they all sang with gusto: "Ain't gonna let no policeman turn us around! . . . Gonna keep on a' testin' . . . 'til we get to freedom's land!"

Gail reported:

We drove straight back to the Whirly-Dip where the kids were served ice cream at the formerly all-white window. Then, just to make sure that Officer Williams knew that traffic tickets and high bail wouldn't stop us, we went to a couple more counters where we were pretty sure they would call the police.

Then we all went home and ate Thanksgiving Dinner.

✦ ✦ ✦

The next day brought new challenges. Luke wrote: "It was like a scene from Kafka [because] there we were in jail, the entire COFO staff, charged with a crime we knew nothing about."

Earlier in the day, Gail and Luke had been getting ready to pick up six high school students who'd gone out testing. While they were standing beside the car in front of the new COFO office where they'd just moved, two officers walked up to them.

"I'm Raymond Davis," one declared. He was the sheriff of Lauderdale County. "A record player was stolen by a man named Cummiskey. He claims it's in your office. Give us the keys so we can open the door."

"We don't have a key," Gail replied.

"You better tell us who has the key or else we'll break down the door!"

Gail asked to see the warrant, but the officers refused. Gail explained that she and Luke couldn't trust white southerners like them unless they were shown a warrant. Grudgingly, one of the officers pulled it out of his pocket.

At this point, their civil rights coworker Sandy Watts walked up.

She explained, "We can't get into the office. Joe Morse has the only key, and he isn't here." Pausing a moment, she added, "Cummiskey told me he wanted to give the record player to COFO as a present. He said he was leaving town."

Gail and Luke stepped into the car, expecting to pick up the waiting teenagers, but Sheriff Davis boomed, "You're not going anywhere. Turn off that motor!"

Gail looked up, pleading, "But the parents of the teens are waiting for us to drive them home. They won't know what's happening and will be worried sick."

The sheriff frowned. "OK," he relented, "but just you. No one else. And you—" he glared, "you come straight back to the police station, ya hear?"

Gail agreed and drove off.

The two officers herded Luke and the others into the police station. In his notes, Luke recounted:

> We were all frisked and fingerprinted and locked up in the cells for White Men and White Women. And in those jail cells we sang freedom songs and talked about our lives.
>
> I heard a train come roaring by and it sounded like freedom roaring away in the night far away from Mississippi.

Soon afterward, police brought twenty-one-year-old, red-haired Joe Morse and his coworker Louise Somlyo to the station. The police had stopped them just before they were able to drive past the town line. Joe was a fellow northern volunteer who was working along with Louise on voter registration and organizing the Mississippi Freedom Democratic Party.

When Gail arrived at the police station, she asked, "What am I charged with?" but was given no answer. She wrote: "I was taken to the 'White Women Only' cell where Louise, Judy, and Sandy were all cheerfully singing Freedom Songs. In the cell next door Eric, Frank, Joe, and Luke were singing too.... Judy found she had her harmonica and we took turns playing that for a while." The four women talked to each other in their cell, piecing together the story of the theft.

Cummiskey was a frequent visitor at the COFO office. He told them he was a sailor from New York, stationed at the nearby Navy base.

Once he admitted to Louise, "I like to steal things, especially from people in the South because I despise them."

Hearing this, Sandy sighed regretfully. "And to think I just believed him when he said he was being discharged and wanted to donate a record player to COFO. So much for trust."

At about ten o'clock, the four men were transferred from the holding cell at the police station to the city jail down the street. The situation there felt more ominous. According to Luke:

Eric, Frank, Joe and I were placed in a cell with a bunch of drunken white prisoners—thieves, tough guys, bitter segregationists.

There were bars on the windows, a toilet without a seat, and a few beds. Every bed was occupied, and I decided that rather than share a bed . . . I would sleep on a hard, green bench.

Meanwhile, back at the police station, the women were being taunted. Gail described the situation: "Several policemen came and called us things like 'N----r-loving bitches'. . . . [Then they] closed the door to the outer hall—telling us it was to 'keep out the stink.' We thanked them."

Before midnight, two police officers came to the white-women-only cell to say that everyone except Sandy was free to leave.

Judy, reluctant to leave Sandy alone, turned to her. "Do you want one of us to stay with you?"

Suddenly, the gate slammed shut with a loud bang.

"All right, damn you, spend the whole night!" one of the cops shouted.

Later, in the wee hours of the night, a cop woke them up.

"Someone else needs the bed," he announced curtly, flapping his hand. "You've got to leave."

But he pointed at Sandy. "She stays! The rest of you, *get out!*"

Around the same time, over at the city jail, Luke and two of his friends were released, but they were forced to leave Joe behind.

Saturday, the next morning, Sandy Watts was charged with burglary. Her bond was set at twenty-five hundred dollars. Joe Morse was charged with receiving stolen property, and his bond was fifteen hundred dollars. Their trial would be on Wednesday, December 2, four days away. Unable to pay bond, Sandy immediately went on a hunger strike. Luke wrote: "The *Meridian Star* has gleefully announced the news. Joe is in jail with a bunch of tough, white segregationist criminals, and I am afraid for him."

After being released from jail in the wee hours of the night, Gail was unable to sleep for long. The trial for her traffic violation, the "wrong turn," was scheduled for that afternoon.

◆ ◆ ◆

At traffic court, Gail pleaded not guilty. She described the proceedings: "First the city gave its case. Acting as city attorney was a smooth-talking, tall cigar-smoking lawyer who wore sunglasses and reminded me more of an automobile salesman than a lawyer. Officer Williams was the only city witness."

Seizing the opportunity to cross-examine the witness, Gail took center stage. She wrote later, with satisfaction, that it "turned into a good show."

She put Officer Williams back on the witness stand. "How long were you following me?"

Although he kept objecting, declaring that her question was irrelevant, Gail was able to prove her point that the officer had been stalking them.

In self-defense, she proclaimed, "This is a *civil rights case* and *not* a traffic violation. I have been arrested not because I am guilty but to prevent me from testing the Civil Rights Bill."

Next, Gail called Judy to the witness stand. Judy corroborated her story.

At the end of her testimony, Judy spontaneously added, "And that left turn in question? It was properly made. It was *not* a traffic violation!"

Gail took the witness stand now in her own defense. Luke watched from the back of the room and observed: "The prosecuting attorney . . . made wisecracks while a chorus of policemen behind him cackled."

Trying to be fair, Judge Neville fined Gail twelve dollars.

She responded politely, "Thank you, Judge, for your leniency, but I will not pay any money because I did *not* commit a crime."

Gail insisted that instead she would serve her sentence in jail. Everyone in the courtroom was shocked.

"They had not expected that," she reported, "and after a second's hesitation, they said, 'OK, lock her up!'"

✦ ✦ ✦

Over Thanksgiving, at home in Rhode Island, we were blissfully unaware that Luke and his friends were rotating in and out of jail. Mom and Al spent hours together engrossed in conversations about literature. Dad floated in and out in his customary way, most of the time secluded upstairs in his study, reading. He pulled me aside a few times to ask how I was liking college and was glad to hear I was adjusting well and enjoying my courses.

It was heartwarming to see Bubbe engaged in her usual routines, moving slowly and deliberately through her day. Mostly, she occupied herself in the kitchen, cooking and cleaning up after us, but each afternoon, she took time out to sit on the couch in the living room and read her Yiddish newspaper. Bubbe had never learned how to read English. *The Forverts*, known in English as the *Daily Jewish Forward*, came to her by mail. I was always fond of seeing the Yiddish script, which looked foreign to me and therefore exotic. Because the couch was deep and soft, stuffed with goose down feathers, Bubbe would often call us for help to stand up.

The day after Thanksgiving, Alix and I took our boyfriends on a long walk along the beach. Alix identified different kinds of seagulls, ducks, and other birds that flew by. The boys found it challenging to keep up with us, unaccustomed as they were to bounding across rocks. My sister and I were like mountain goats in familiar terrain.

During the holiday break at home, we didn't pay close attention to the news, but we did discuss a few articles in the *New York Times* related to the continuing investigation of the murders and to other civil rights arrests and disturbances around the state of

Mississippi. For the most part, however, the news was like a steady drumbeat in the background.

Then, on Sunday morning, just as Al and I were getting ready to leave, we found an article by reporter Homer Bigart in which he addressed the question, Why had the Klan chosen Mickey Schwerner as their target? Bigart learned from a moderate local white leader that up to fifty Klan members had conspired to murder him. "'Schwerner wore a beard and looked very Jewish,' explained one Philadelphian. 'He had become a known figure to the Klan; he had been in the area several months.'"

Although this news was not unexpected, the report was chilling.

✦ ✦ ✦

Meanwhile, in Meridian, Sandy Watts and Joe Morse were now being held in the county jail since they were awaiting trial. Gail was serving out her sentence in a holding cell at the police station. Because white women were rarely jailed in Meridian, there was no cell assigned to them at the city jail. Instead, they were kept at the nearby police station. The holding cell, located in a hallway directly behind the main desk, provided no privacy, which was a mixed blessing. On the one hand, police officers kept coming by and leering, but on the other hand, because it was out in the open, visitors were able to drop by.

Each day, the city jail delivered Gail's lunches, wrapped in brown paper. Lacking supplies, Gail considered the remnants of her lunch wrappings precious. She saved them to write letters to her friends in the North, one of whom was Portia.

White Women Only
    December 1, 1964
    Dear Portia, I just ate a green pepper which Luke brought me because I wanted something fresh and green. . . . [T]hese days [in jail] have been good days. It has been the first vacation I've

had in months . . . most important for a vacation, no responsibili-
ties to anyone.

Gail laid out the reasons behind her decision to be jailed instead
of paying the fine.

> It seems that the only way we can put pressure on the city to stop
> these harassment fines is to start going to jail for them.
>   . . .[I]f the city undertakes to give me food, clean sheets, blan-
> kets, a shower, towels, bathroom facilities, heat, and a room to
> myself where I can catch up on some reading, writing, thinking,
> and sleeping— I am not going to object. It will cost them more
> than $12.00 before the four days are up.

On at least one of his visits, Luke brought students along. From
behind bars, Gail learned what was happening in their lives in
the outside world. She told them about essays she was reading by
Henry David Thoreau on civil disobedience. She also explained
why she was in jail, and in this way, Freedom School continued.

Chapter 20

CONTRIBUTION TO THE DELINQUENCY OF MINORS

Around the same time as these events, the principal at Harris High School spied some Freedom School students wearing MFDP buttons. This violated a school rule that made the display of political slogans or signs taboo. When told to remove their buttons, most students complied but not Willie Clark or Bettye Manual. When they refused, the principal suspended them from school for a day. Returning to school, however, they still wore their buttons because they viewed them as an expression of free speech. Unfortunately, the principal would not bend, so they were permanently expelled from school. Although Bettye and Willie were fiercely proud, this was a major blow. Neither one had a family able to intervene on their behalf to get them reinstated by school authorities. Nor could they afford private schools. Without hesitation, COFO staff took responsibility. They decided there had to be a way to help these bright, passionate, young activists graduate from high school. The search was on.

✦ ✦ ✦

Early Friday morning on December 4 in Rhode Island, our parents sat down as usual at the kitchen table to eat breakfast. They soon settled into reading the *New York Times*. They were unprepared for a headline that appeared on page 20, which immediately caught their attention. Homer Bigart was reporting again from Meridian.

MISSISSIPPI TEST LEADS TO ARRESTS:
8 Negro Children Seized after Restaurant Visit
by Homer Bigart
Meridian, Miss., Dec. 3, 1964

Two white civil rights workers from New England drove a carload of "freedom school" youths to the Toddle House, a local restaurant, in a test of compliance with the Civil Rights Act last night.

All were arrested. The civil rights workers, Freeman Cocroft, 22 years old, of Providence, RI, who was graduated last June from Yale, and Lucian [*sic*] Kabat, 25, of Saunderstown, RI, a medical student at Stanford University, were given a preliminary arraignment today on charges of contribution to the delinquency of minors.

They pleaded not guilty. Bail was set at $650 each.

Here, Lucien was mentioned by name, as well as his good friend Freeman. They were arrested no less and on quite serious charges!

"Contributing to the delinquency of minors?!" Dad gasped, simultaneously bewildered and unsurprised. "And Nunc," he added, calling Mom by the affectionate nickname he used, "look what it says here—bail, $650! What's going to happen to him now? What can we do?"

Mom grabbed the paper from his hand and scanned the article as quickly as she could. Then, to make sure she understood, she went back to the heading and began reading it aloud. Bubbe sat down to listen too, her face sagging, contorted with worry. Mom continued to read the next section.

Negro Children Freed

...Judge Harwell...warned staff members of [COFO]...that they faced "serious trouble" if they continued to "lead innocent little people into trouble in the middle of the night."

...Judge Harwell warned the children, "We've been enjoying a lot of peace and tranquility down here and we will not countenance any trouble. I feel you were led into this by adults."

✦ ✦ ✦

Early in the morning, while these newspapers were being distributed, Luke was scribbling. "I am writing this letter from the Meridian jail. Last night, Freeman and I drove a carload of nine ...high school students to the A&W Root Beer Stand. As the teens approached, two white teenagers screamed, 'The n-----s is integratin'—The n-----s is integratin'!' [Then] they locked the door and called the police."

All the teens quickly got back in the car, and Luke drove on to the Toddle House Diner. On the way, they passed four police cars. At this second stop, Luke and Free stayed back with one girl in the parked car. The other eight teenagers stepped inside the restaurant to order cokes to see if they'd be served. While the teens were testing inside the diner, carloads of local toughs began arriving. Soon, a crowd gathered in the parking lot.

Luke and Free agreed it would be wise for Free to get out of the car to call the COFO office and report on the darkening situation. While Free went to look for a phone booth, Luke and the girl stayed behind. Luke described the scene:

One car pulled in front of us, one on the side and one behind, and we were boxed in. I rolled up the windows and locked the doors. An ugly crowd gathered around the car and cruel sneering faces leered at us through the window.

... They were hollering ... "N----r lover, you're going to get what Schwerner got. You son of a bitch." ... They shouted cruel and obscene things at her.

They shined bright flashlights in my face. I was terrified. I have never seen human faces with such an animal look, and I will never forget them.

I looked at [her] and said, "We shall overcome"—she answered, "We shall overcome." I kept wondering, "Where are those four carloads of policemen?"

The eight teens emerged from the diner and took in the scene. Holding their heads high, they walked bravely through the crowd and got into the car. Suddenly, Free walked up from behind the crowd and made his way straight to the car door. "I think the crowd was stupefied by his courage," Luke noted. "No one made a move to restrain him."

Just as Luke started the motor, a man appeared at the window. Wearing a brown suit, he looked official.

He roared, "If you try to get away, I'll have to shoot you!"

Luke immediately shut off the engine and stared at the key, afraid to look up. Everyone else in the car dropped their heads and cowered.

The man turned around to face the crowd, yelling, "Look! I don't like this any more than you do, but if you bother them, I'll have to arrest you."

He turned back to the car window. "Now get going!"

Luke wrote later, "My legs were shaking, but I managed to drive through the crowd to the COFO office, followed by a carload of toughs."

At the COFO office, Luke and Free were just beginning to breathe again when they learned that another group of teenagers had gone out testing at the Trailways Bus Station. These teens were stuck without a ride back.

Nodding to each other, Luke volunteered, "We'll fetch them."

As Luke was driving to the bus station, Free spotted a police car approaching in the opposite lane. Lo and behold! There were their teenagers packed into the backseat. Luke promptly turned around and followed. At the police station, the teens were booked with disorderly conduct.

On entering the station, Free made an unusual request.

"Arrest me too!" he declared, raising his arms in the air as if to surrender.

"And me too!" echoed Luke.

The police, it turned out, were more than happy to oblige. For the "crime" of helping teens test the Civil Rights Act, which was, after all, the law of the land, Luke and Freeman were charged with several different offenses. The police just couldn't make up their minds, it seemed, until they finally settled on the crime of contributing to the delinquency of minors.

While being led to their jail cell, Luke inquired, "Free, why did you volunteer to go to jail?"

"It was the only thing I could honorably do."

Luke concurred. "I feel the same."

Luke and Free were placed together in a tiny holding cell at the police station. To buoy their spirits, they sang freedom songs. Luke jotted notes that he would later add to a letter. "The cell walls are lined with trails of spit and the usual bathroom wall philosophies. . . . We wanted the kids to know we were with them and were outraged by the events of the evening. We weren't going to abandon them." At five o'clock in the morning, Free and Luke were awakened abruptly and transferred to the Meridian City Jail.

Locked in the "white-men-only" cell, they found themselves in close quarters with a group of tough-looking characters. "We didn't say a word to the prisoners," Luke explained. "Had they known we were civil rights workers or even Northerners they might have tried to hurt us." Falling asleep on a filthy sheet spotted with blood, Luke wondered about the former prisoner who

The Meridian City Jail. Courtesy of Syrtiller Kabat.

Luke wrote in his scrapbook: "We used to drive by and holler 'Freedom.' And we spent fearful hours in the segregated "white" cell on the 2nd floor."

had left this trace. *What was his story?* And the blood—*Was it tuberculosis or was he beaten?*

Later that morning, Luke and Free were transferred yet again, this time to the county jail for the preliminary arraignment. Entering the jail, they heard the teens singing in the distance. "Oh Freedom!" Luke was deeply moved. "I have rarely heard a more beautiful sound."

At the preliminary arraignment, as reported in the *New York Times*, Luke and Free faced Judge Harwell, and each one pleaded not guilty. The judge read the charge against them—contributing to the delinquency of minors—and set their bail at $650 each. He gave them a continuance, and they were placed in a new cell at the county jail.

✦ ✦ ✦

Meanwhile, in the early morning back in Rhode Island, Mom continued reading the *New York Times* article out loud and came to the subheading "Angry Crowd Gathers." She stiffened but kept reading.

> At the [COFO] council headquarters, a spokesman said that Mr. Cocroft and Mr. Kabat had taken the children on a tour of white restaurants to test whether Negroes would be served.
>
> . . . An angry white crowd gathered outside the restaurant. . . .
>
> . . . [T]he two men took the children to a nearby bus station where a few minutes later the police arrested all of the group except Mr. Kabat.

At this point, Bubbe released an audible sigh of relief.

Mom continued, "Mr. Kabat, a teacher at the Freedom School, went to police headquarters *and demanded to be arrested.*"

When Mom finished reading this sentence, she stopped.

She looked up at Dad and Bubbe, bug-eyed. Mom put the paper down and didn't finish reading the last three paragraphs. What she had read aloud was sufficient. The three of them froze for a long moment and stared at each other in silence. As soon as they unfroze, they became hysterical. Dad left in a flurry for his day's work in Providence, filled with apprehension. Mom and Dad agreed they'd stay in close touch by phone.

✦ ✦ ✦

In their new cell at the county jail, Luke and Free felt safer than they had before. Although they still assumed their cellmates were diehard segregationists, they decided to break their silence. They found that the men were segregationists, as they suspected, but their reaction was surprising. Luke wrote: "We told some of the other prisoners we were COFO workers and discussed our differences of opinion about Negroes." Luke discovered that he and Free could talk openly with these men about their differing views of segregation without a fierce argument ensuing and feeling endangered.

As soon as one of the prisoners learned that Luke was studying medicine, he confided, "I'm very worried. My heart's bad. They're not giving me the medicine I need, and my symptoms keep getting worse. Can you help me?"

"You must assert yourself," Luke replied. "Demand that the jailer bring you the medicine you need, and I'll back you up. Can you do this?"

For Luke, it was a matter of principle. He felt the obligation inherent in his profession to doctor anyone in need. After all, he'd pledged to uphold the Hippocratic oath as a medical student, "to treat the ill to the best of my ability." Providing care as a doctor overrode any repugnance he harbored toward the man's segregationist views.

Another prisoner in their cell was a colorful old character named Pat McCarthy. "[He] told us, 'I'm a professional thief. Never worked a day in my life. I made $50 a day and support dope addicts on my earnings.' He was going through withdrawal symptoms. I told him about Synanon, a community of dope addicts who help each other get clean, and he was interested." Pat McCarthy was loquacious. He mentioned that before Luke and Free had arrived, their friend and fellow COFO worker—Joe Morse—had been locked in this very same cell. The record player thief, Cummiskey, had been here, too.

Confined together, Cummiskey realized how his not taking personal responsibility for his crime was leading to dire consequences for Joe and Sandy. Cummiskey decided to write a statement declaring that Joe Morse and Sandy Watts had had nothing to do with the burglary. He had committed the crime by himself, aided and abetted by no one else. His confession would be worthless, however, without the signatures of two witnesses. The only witnesses available were the other prisoners in the jail cell. At first, no one stepped forward to sign as a witness, but Pat McCarthy struggled with the decision.

Pat admitted with chagrin, "I just couldn't let that boy Joe take Cummiskey's rap. Even though I hated to, I signed that statement."

Luke was amazed to hear Pat tell this story because, as he wrote, they were "all segregationists who would like to get even with COFO." Pat, the thief, also explained to Luke and Free how he had come to Joe's defense earlier on. In the cell, as soon as they realized Joe was a civil rights worker, three young toughs had threatened to beat him up. Pat stood up for Joe.

He spoke boldly to the jailer: "If this boy is beaten, your police force will catch hell!"

Pat McCarthy abided by a clear code of honor, and this had a transformative effect on Luke. "I was surprised that although my cellmates were criminals and segregationists, they were just men." He dubbed Pat McCarthy "a segregationist with a heart," reflecting with gratitude and relief that "Joe and Sandy were released from jail today."

It was because of the thief Pat McCarthy that Homer Bigart's *New York Times* article concluded with these paragraphs:

In the same court today [Dec. 3] Judge Harwell fined Joe Morse, a council worker from Dakota, Minn. $150, and Sandra Watts, another staff member from Lakeview, Ore., $250.

Both were arrested last week in a raid on COFO headquarters in which the police found a stolen record player.

On Tuesday, Vincent Cummiskey, 18, a former sailor who had been arrested for the theft of the record player from a local apartment, pleaded guilty to two counts of willful trespass and was fined $500 on each count.

✦ ✦ ✦

Away at college in Rochester, I was not reading news reports. I felt overloaded enough just keeping up with my assignments for reading books and writing papers. For this reason, I was not aware of what was unfolding in Meridian. But the pace of events there did not let up. In fact, things kept accelerating.

Chapter 21

CLOSE QUARTERS

On this one day, December 4, Luke and Free had already experienced a sleepless night shuffled between jail cells in three locations. Then, in the wee hours of the morning, they'd faced Judge Harwell at their preliminary hearing. Afterward, they were transferred to a cell in the county jail where they felt relaxed enough to chat with their cellmates. The day was now slipping by, and it was afternoon. Luke overheard a report. "Someone in jail has a radio. . . . 20 men have been arrested for the murder of Chaney, Schwerner and Goodman. About twelve of them came from Meridian. The radio said that these men are in the Meridian Jail. Free and I looked at each other and laughed very nervously." A bit later, Luke crossed paths with some of the men. "I met 5 men and was told they were among the murderers. Pink-faced businessmen-types in suits who looked like civic leaders. They joked with the jailer and inquired about the food. They acted cocky and confident."

✦ ✦ ✦

What led up to these arrests? Earlier in the fall, one member of the Klan, James Jordan, had agreed to cooperate with the FBI agents who were investigating the crime. Jordan confessed to being involved in the murder. In mid-November, a second Klan member also confessed and offered further details about the shootings. Based on these two confessions, on December 4, federal prosecutors from the US Justice Department arrested the nineteen men identified by the FBI as the murderers, plus two men accused of withholding knowledge of the felony—twenty-one men in all. The men who were residents of Meridian were now being held at the county jail.

How ironic was it that Luke and Free were confined in their cell because they themselves had decided on impulse not to abandon the teenagers? They had begged to be arrested! As Free had said at the time, "It was the only thing I could honorably do," and without hesitation, Luke had agreed with him. The police were, unsurprisingly, more than happy to oblige, and that morning Judge Harwell had officially charged them with the crime of contribution to the delinquency of minors. But now their situation was quickly deteriorating. The bond required for each of them was very costly, and they had no idea how to pay for it. It was Friday afternoon. Soon, government offices would be closing for the weekend.

In his letter, Luke noted that "Free called COFO and warned them that we would be locked in jail with the murderers." And after Free went to make the phone call, Luke reported "the jailer told Free that they will maintain order." Despite these reassuring words, they both remained terribly anxious. Looking around their cramped cell, how could they not but wonder, *Will any of the murderers be placed in here with us? What will happen then?*

✦ ✦ ✦

Back in Rhode Island, excruciating hours passed before Mom heard from Luke. He phoned:

"Mom, I'm in jail here with Free," he began.

"Yes, I know—"

"I need your help. They've got the murderers here too. The men who killed Mickey Schwerner and James and Andy—"

Mom was shaking when she immediately phoned Dad at work. The two of them switched into overdrive. At Luke's suggestion, Dad got in touch with Freeman's parents, and the four parents agreed to work together. They contacted Rhode Island Senator Claiborne Pell and pressured him to help them find a lawyer and a way to pay for bail in Mississippi. Senator Pell was eager to help and played an essential role. At least some of the money for bail was wired late that afternoon. However, by the time the transaction occurred, government offices in Mississippi were closing. Luke and Free remained in jail.

✦ ✦ ✦

Pat McCarthy may have taken some pleasure in adding to Luke and Free's anxiety. He predicted their future at the Hinds County Penal Farm, a local prison where they would be sent when convicted. Although it was a local prison and not Parchman Prison, the most notorious Mississippi state prison, this prospect was fearful enough.

Pat warned them, perhaps slyly, "You'll be beaten by the jailers and the prisoners at the County Farm."

A civil rights lawyer came over the weekend to consult with Luke and Free. He suggested that he would try to swing a deal. He proposed that each of them would pay a fine of one hundred dollars in return for a guilty plea. Then Luke confronted a dilemma: "A guilty plea offends my sense of justice and working on a chain gang at the County Farm offends my sense of self-preservation. This is a very difficult situation."

✦ ✦ ✦

Adding insult to injury, the US Justice Department could not actually charge the accused with the crime of murder. Murder is rarely a federal crime and only if it occurs on federal property. Otherwise, the crime of murder is covered by state laws. The FBI hoped that

the state of Mississippi would prosecute the case, but the day after
the arrest of the twenty-one men, the *New York Times* reported:

> Sunday December 6
>
> Mississippi authorities declined today to take immediate action
> against the men arrested by the Federal Bureau of Investigation in
> connection with the slaying of three civil rights workers.
>
> . . . After the state officials declined to do so, the bureau proceeded
> with the Federal Charges.

Federal prosecutors had to resort to a workaround. Instead of
murder, nineteen men were charged with "conspiring to violate
the civil rights of Schwerner, Chaney, and Goodman," and the
remaining two, with "refusing to provide information about the
murders." White Mississippians from around the state immediately
rallied to the side of the accused. They organized a defense fund to
pay for all their legal expenses. As a first order of business, bail was
paid to the tune of over one hundred thousand dollars to cover all
of them. "Justice" in Mississippi was topsy-turvy, to say the least.

On Sunday, the accused murderers were freed under bond,
pending their preliminary hearing scheduled for Thursday. Behind
bars, Luke, Free, and their fellow prisoners were in the dark. Not
one of them was told, so no one realized, that the accused murderers had been released under bond and had left the jail. Thus,
Luke and Free continued on high alert within a cloud of anxiety.

On Monday morning, adding to this distressing situation, Free
was handed a warrant. In addition to the original charge, he now
found himself accused of grand larceny. This is a theft of such
magnitude that it constitutes a felony. How was this possible?
Stunned, Luke asked to see the warrant.

> It was so absurd that I laughed when I saw it—and so did Free—
> but we both realize that this is a serious matter. They have made a
> mockery of justice and used it as a weapon of intimidation.

They obstructed testing of the Civil Rights Bill and stood by while a mob threatened our lives, and then when we asked to go to jail as a demonstration of our indignation, they trumped up charges of loitering, disturbing the peace, contribution to the delinquency of minors, and now Grand Larceny!

The situation was gruesome.

Luke and Free had been arrested on Thursday evening, December 3. It was now four days later. They had both been charged with a serious crime: contribution to the delinquency of minors. Money had been sent from the North to pay for their bail, but they had not been released. They believed that the accused murderers were still in the same jail and at any moment they might find themselves sharing the cell with one or more of them. Having lived under the shadow of the heinous "Neshoba County crime" all summer long, Luke and Free had observed firsthand the devastating impact it brought upon the children and the community they had come to love. They had just read a warrant issued for Freeman's arrest on charges of grand larceny. What else could go wrong?

At this point, the jailer approached their cell to announce that he was ready to release Luke, but not Freeman. Free would have to stay locked up because of the grand larceny charge against him. Looking over at him, Luke was beside himself.

"Are you kidding? I can't leave you all alone in this jail with the white murderers of Chaney, Schwerner and Goodman!"

The phone rang. The sheriff was calling.

The jailer turned to them. "Well, umm . . . There's been a sort of . . . umm . . . mistake. The grand larceny is for someone named Crawford . . . umm—" His voice dropped, now almost a whisper, "Not Cocroft."

Glory be! Freeman Cocroft—what a fine name! Not to be confused with anyone else's, for goodness sake!

Luke and Free left jail together. Blessedly, they had not been forced to share a jail cell with the murderers.

As they walked down the street and peered up at the sky, Free remarked with a twinkle in his eye, "You realize, of course, it was just a jail *within* a jail."

"Yeah, sure," Luke replied, looking around at the dusty red clay dirt, the beat-up sidewalks, and the old buildings around them. "But I'm mighty happy to leave that dark iron world behind and be out here now in the sunshine and the fresh air of the 'Great Jail of Mississippi.'"

✦ ✦ ✦

On Monday night, when Mom and Dad finally reached me by phone at my dorm in Rochester, I was surprised to hear them both sounding buoyant given the grim tale they were telling. But it was clear that they both felt relief, as if they too had just been released from jail. I assumed they realized this was only a temporary, although welcome, reprieve, as long as Luke remained in Meridian. I was aghast when they told me how he'd been in the same jail as the murderers.

Mom and Dad's excited words spilled over each other as they both spoke at once. It was confusing.

Finally, I interrupted. "Is Luke alright?"

"Yes," Mom reassured me, "as far as we know."

I was disappointed that they had so few details to share. It was obvious Luke hadn't had the chance to tell them very much about it. When they hung up, questions lingered. I knew Luke probably possessed neither money nor time to call me at the dorm. Besides, I was out a lot and would be hard to reach. My calling him wasn't possible either. No one had given me the phone number for the COFO office, and I only had access to pay phones. How many quarters would it take to call an unidentified number in Mississippi? I'd have to wait for answers.

Chapter 22

BITTER PILL

In the days that followed, Luke took time to consider his recent, terrifying experience in jail in light of the more idealistic thoughts he'd entertained previously. Before, he'd treated being confined in a jail cell almost as a breeze. Soon after he had met Judy Wright some weeks ago, she had told him about being a Freedom Rider in 1961. Luke was captivated. Her experience in the notorious Parchman Prison impressed him deeply.

Judy explained that when she applied, she was warned of the risks she would face. During the initial interview, she was questioned: "Are you aware of what jail in Mississippi is like, especially for someone doing what you're planning to do? You will be under the thumb of people who hate you."

In her memoir, *Acts of Resistance*, Judy stated, "I knew when I bought that bus ticket for Jackson, I was buying a ticket for jail."

Luke admired Judy's courage. After hearing her story, he wrote in his diary: "She was locked up in the State Penitentiary for 5 weeks, and she dreamed of motion, that she was waltzing about, and she dreamed of cake.... Her story reminded me of the German folksong 'Die Gedanken Sind Frei.'" In the song, no matter what happens to you—even within prison walls, you can remain free in the mind. So says the title, "Thoughts Are Free."

When Gail chose to serve out her sentence in jail rather than pay a fine for a "traffic violation," Luke wrote: "I'm very proud of Gail. She is in jail now and she is one of the world's freest persons."

But after mulling over his own recent experience in jail, he confessed:

> I have heard a lot of talk about freedom of the mind in prison but I really must admit that my thoughts in jail did not fly far beyond a wish to stretch muscles and see the sunshine, to protect myself from the other prisoners, to get back to the Freedom School and see the kids.
>
> It's sort of a psychosomatic thing. When the body is cramped, the mind dreams of freedom, but it dwells on freedom of motion and in this way, it is cramped.

✦ ✦ ✦

Meanwhile, the preliminary hearing for the nineteen accused murderers was set for Thursday, which was fast approaching. The case against the two accomplices, arrested for withholding information from the FBI, would be handled separately. The night before the hearing, the civil rights community gathered for a meeting at Mount Olive Church. Mrs. Chaney designed the program to prepare everyone for the hearing. Spiritual in nature, it featured a silent prayer for justice.

Reverend J. R. Porter offered the invocation. "No matter what happens at the hearing tomorrow, whether or not you agree with it, it is God's will."

Luke reacted. "In the background the organ moaned and groaned the strains of a hymn, and I groaned silently to myself. In my silent Prayer, I wondered whether Justice would be done." Under the circumstances, he questioned one of his long-held principles. "I hate capital punishment, but I found myself thinking that perhaps in Mississippi such a terrible punishment would be an effective deterrent."

At the end of the meeting the community broke into a song, adding their own words. "We've been buked and we've been scorned— / We have hung our heads and cried / For those like the three who died, / We shall overcome."

✦ ✦ ✦

The next day, December 10, the hearing began in court. John Doar, a tall, dignified, and experienced lawyer, was the special prosecutor assigned by the US Justice Department. Along with his assistant attorney, Robert Owen, they presented the FBI's case. Doar's goal was to secure indictments against eighteen of the men in order to bring them to trial. The accused men sat in the jury box on chairs lined up against the back wall.

Luke observed the proceedings. "I looked hard at each face for a sign of guilt or a trace of humanity. But the faces were dumb, and they were smiling, perhaps nervously, but malignantly with apparent confidence—swaggering, cocky, painful smiles."

Their defense attorneys were aggressive. When one of them addressed the prosecutors, remarking, "We don't believe you have any proof," the accused men began to snicker.

Luke found it painful to watch the proceedings and wrote:

The hearing was sickening. . . .

There was a recess for lunch and when we returned to the courthouse, only segregationists ("friends and relatives of the defendants") were admitted to the Courtroom. Even Mrs. Chaney was barred from the hearing.

Esther Carter, the US Commissioner for the Southern District of Mississippi who was hearing the case, promptly dismissed the charges against the men. She claimed the signed confession that was obtained and read on the witness stand by an FBI agent was only hearsay.

To no avail, government attorney Robert Owen argued that hearsay evidence was permissible in a preliminary hearing like this one. "Agent testimony is used in every district in the country."

A mere fifteen minutes elapsed before a newspaperman emerged from the hearing room, announcing, "It's all over. They've been released."

The nineteen men sauntered out of the courtroom, all smiles, congratulating each other. Round one, for them, was a victory.

Luke penned:

> Mrs. Heidelberg began to cry and screamed something about judgment and the Lord—and Mrs. Chaney cried, but quietly so nobody could see.
>
> . . . TV cameras focused in on the Chaneys in their grief and fury. Flashbulbs were popping, and we walked to the COFO office singing, "Oh Freedom" and "We Shall Overcome."

Esther Carter's judgment—dropping the charges—was a very bitter pill to swallow. It provided further proof, if any was needed, that in Mississippi, in Luke's words, "murder is legal."

Unknown to everyone else, John Doar and his team knew they had more convincing evidence they could reveal, but they had decided, strategically, not to do so at this point.

Instead, at the end of the court hearing, Robert Owen stated, "I request that a grand jury be called as soon as possible."

✦ ✦ ✦

That night, Luke was feeling very disheartened. "I spoke with a Negro man in a bar. He was bitter and said, 'There is nothing for us now but violence.' I tried to talk to him about nonviolence. I said that nonviolence is a way of fighting and not really a passive thing."

But the man replied, "How long will it take for this political action to help me?"

Listening to his plea, Luke realized with chagrin that "generations may have to die in this prison of segregation before there's democracy in Mississippi."

The man continued, "A band of Negro vigilantes could make justice by taking Sheriff Rainey's life. We Negroes could show the White Man we won't longer be buked and scorned."

In his diary, Luke confessed: "It was hard for me to argue with him. He may be right."

Here again arose the perennial question of using guns versus nonviolence. Luke was aware that he and the other civil rights activists were being protected by Blacks in the community who did have guns and were willing to use them in self-defense. The threat they posed to white Klansmen helped to create a boundary of safety, which allowed the civil rights activists to remain nonviolent. It was a paradox: the threat of violence made nonviolence possible.

Chapter 23

NONVIOLENCE 2

In Meridian, within the civil rights community, the question of nonviolence hung in the air and called for constant rethinking. Like those dedicated to the Buddhist practice of mindfulness, each practitioner of nonviolence needed to stay present, focused, and alert. And a related question functioned as one's constant companion: *Am I doing the right thing?*

After the harrowing events of the past two weeks, Luke pondered the question of nonviolence and kept circling back to it again and again. He gathered together not only his own thoughts about nonviolence but also those of students and other teachers at the Freedom School. He sifted through papers he'd saved, seeking answers and wanting to better understand his own evolving thoughts.

For one assignment, Freedom School students had written essays in response to the question, Will nonviolence work in Mississippi? Their answers were deeply personal. Luke reread an essay by fourteen-year-old Suponie and saw that she agreed with the man in the bar.

She wrote: "People are always talking about Nonviolence, Nonviolence. If you don't fight back, who will?"

In contrast, her classmate Merline Jimerson considered the issue from both sides. "I feel that they would respect us more if we were non-violent. . . . [P]eople usually would much rather talk things out than to use violence. . . . But if the KKK wanted to attack us, I believe I'd use guns on them first before consulting the use of non-violence." Merline concluded her essay by upholding the principle of nonviolence while simultaneously voicing her predicament. "But sometimes I wonder, what other alternative have we?"

The man in the bar had led Luke to wonder about the same thing. Perhaps it would take generations, Luke had thought to himself. The insight was very unsettling. Was there an alternative? Questions abounded.

Wasn't resorting to violence always wrong? Was there another path that could speed up the process of change? What was the likelihood of a positive outcome, of ending segregation once and for all?

Luke was particularly struck when he reread an essay by student Dorothy Clayton.

Nonviolence all around is probably the best way out. Killing never solve anything. . . . [But] take me for example. If I go downtown and demonstrate and a white person hit me, see, I couldn't take it. I would hit that person back because you see I have a high temper. I might happen to hurt one of them. So let it stay nonviolence and I will be happy with it.

Luke wrote in his journal that Dorothy's answer was "very honest [because] I feel that many 'nonviolent people' must fear their own capacity for violence and they seek to control their violent feelings through this philosophy." Like Dorothy Clayton, he was quick to anger. He found it hard to restrain his hot temper and therefore felt great sympathy for her quandary.

Nonviolence was a challenging, spiritual practice. It required an amazing level of self-control. Perhaps this is why Mahatma Gandhi had referred to nonviolence as a "weapon of the strong." Gandhi had set the bar especially high by expecting his followers to confront hatred and conquer any opponent with love. But is this ideal too far out of reach for most people? For almost all of us?

Nonviolence, in both theory and practice, posed other challenges as well. Luke conceded: "I find it hard to love mankind in the abstract and when I hear talk of Nonviolence and love for the enemy, I find it hard to accept.... It seems most honest to me to use Nonviolence as a tactic rather than philosophy." Although idealism and the concept of nonviolence were what had first inspired Luke to volunteer for Freedom Summer, actual experience was changing his perspective. It proved to be love for individual people, rather than belief in an abstract concept, that now bound him to the cause and motivated nonviolent action.

> I thought of the Memphis orientation and how they presented us with the question, "Is your commitment to civil rights so strong that you are willing to die for it?" The question then was abstract and unreal for me. At the time I didn't know any of the Negro people of Meridian. Had I known Mrs. Heidelberg and Reverend Culpepper, and the kids of the Community Center and my freedom school students, I would have come to Mississippi without hesitation for I love them and care for them.

Luke was not alone in this transformation. Direct experience was always the most powerful teacher, and many other volunteers underwent a similar change of heart.

Caring so deeply for the individuals he knew in Meridian made it hard, yet again, for Luke to rip himself away from his friends. But his medical studies required it. Before long, he would return to Stanford.

Chapter 24

BRIEF INTERLUDE

For me, the Christmas break provided a welcome change of scene. Al invited me to visit his parents and younger brother, Jerry, at their home in Queens. I had previously stayed in Manhattan with its crowded bustle of people, noise, and thrilling museums, but I had never gone to any of the outer boroughs. This would be my first taste of suburbia.

Al's mother, Lena, belonged to a large Sephardic family that had immigrated from Turkey in the early 1900s. Instead of Yiddish based on German, she grew up speaking Ladino, a version of Spanish. I was eager to learn Ladino folksongs, a heritage of music I hadn't heard of. Lena's relatives—Al's countless cousins, aunts, and uncles—traipsed in and out of the house at all hours, loud and brusque like the New Yorkers they were. To escape the noisy, cramped, and smoke-filled rooms, I took frequent walks around the neighborhood.

His father, Max, worked as a presser in a factory in the Garment District on the Lower East Side. He was orphaned as a child and raised by his aunt.

Sitting at the kitchen table, he turned toward me, smiling, and shouted to make sure I could hear me over the din, "I asked her to marry me and look what I got. A bargain! They just took me in."

I was disappointed that I wasn't going to meet Al's identical twin brother, Murray, and his wife, Peggy. They were attending graduate school in Berkeley, California. I was curious to understand more about their twin relationship.

Al's family embraced a more traditional, religious view of Judaism than mine did. The common thread that linked our families was food. Cooking and eating were the order of the day, but the dishes were very different. His mother served up an endless array of Turkish delicacies I found exotic.

Next, I took the train up to Rhode Island, relieved to be back to the freedom of the beach, the bay, and wild woods. Luke and I reconnected by phone.

"So, Luke, you want me to tell you about Al and his family? I'm ready to spill the beans."

"Are you kidding? Of course!"

"Well, he reads all the time, like Mom. He likes to drink coffee and talk about ideas. He can quote poetry and lots of proverbs. Two days after we first went out, he showed up for a master dance class I took with a visiting artist, and he's cute in tights. He wears a gold ring in his left ear, so he looks a bit like a foreigner. He's handsome—deep-set brown eyes. One bad thing, though, he smokes like a fiend, and his breath stinks, so he's not perfect. I guess I can't ask for everything."

Luke had no room to respond until I was completely out of breath. I sensed him smiling.

"Pig, I can't wait to meet him. Your first love. It's an exciting thing."

I was eager to ask, "What happened to you in Mississippi?"

He painted a picture, filling in some of the blanks. But we could only cover so much in a phone conversation. I knew there would be more to come. I longed to see my big brother in person. I think he missed me too. As always, it was hard to say goodbye.

Part Four

OUTCOMES AND CARRYING ON

Chapter 25

A PERIOD OF TURMOIL

Back at medical school, Luke was finding student life and his work with patients rather lonely and colorless in comparison to the tight-knit community of Meridian. He was not the only one dealing with a difficult time of transition. Judy Wright wrote letters to keep him abreast of what was happening. By late January, she sounded downcast. "We really miss you here. . . . [E]veryone is preparing to leave, worst of all, Gail, Bettye, and Willie. Frank is already getting nostalgic about our sitting in Beals [Restaurant] and gabbing with you and Gail. Please write to us, Luke." In December, Willie and Bettye had been expelled from Harris High. Would the teens be able to finish high school? Not without leaving Meridian. Gail and Judy had scrambled to find a solution.

Judy reported that Willie and Bettye would be moving up North—Willie to New York City and Bettye to Newton, a suburb of Boston. "Willie is going to school in New York and will be living in an apartment adjacent to Ken and Pinky [Slote]." The Slotes, who were Freedom Summer volunteers, would watch out for Willie in the bustling Big Apple. Quite a change of scene from Meridian. Through a friend, Gail had found a progressive private school willing to accept Bettye on scholarship. Judy had located a family for her to live with nearby. For the moment, it seemed, the two teens were set, but they both faced a period of adjustment that would be fraught with challenges.

In addition to the letters, Luke was following the news. Prosecutor John Doar had recently been promoted to assistant attorney general for civil rights. As Doar had hoped, he was able to convince a federal grand jury in Jackson, Mississippi's state capital, to issue indictments against the men. They were now dubbed the "Neshoba County conspirators." On January 15, 1965, not long after Luke's return to California, the FBI again arrested the nineteen accused murderers and charged them with the same crime—violating the civil rights of Chaney, Goodman, and Schwerner.

By mid-February, Judy was back in jail and wrote a long letter to Luke. She, Frank, and others were charged with "blocking the sidewalk" while protesting outside a segregated restaurant in the Lamar Hotel. The luncheon to commemorate Anti-Crime Week featured a prominent FBI agent as keynote speaker. Judy and her fellow activists were flummoxed. Why in the world would a federal agent agree to speak at a segregated event? Wasn't this in flagrant disregard of the federal civil rights law? She and Frank, along with thirteen others, marched outside carrying handmade signs. "Today's special at the Lamar Hotel is Jim Crow," read one of them.

> So here I am in jail. Because I am the only white woman, I am alone. . . . [After being charged at the police station] with blocking the sidewalk, everyone else was taken to the city jail. Almost all the men decided to go limp—to have to be dragged around rather than co-operate in any way with injustice . . . Joe Morse . . . Frank . . . Gregg Kaslo . . . Bozo . . . Richard Tinsley. . . .
>
> Lee Roberts, a white policeman, made sure that the bodies of the boys were slammed against the steel lockers.

Luke was all too familiar with policeman Lee Roberts. During the summer, it was he who used to drive his police car slowly by, staring at Luke and Gail on their regular morning walks through his neighborhood on their way to Freedom School. Lee Robert's brother, Alton, was one of the Klansmen arrested for the murders of Schwerner, Chaney, and Goodman. Later, unsurprisingly, it was revealed that Lee Roberts, too, was a member of the Ku Klux Klan.

Although Judy was relieved to be the only one in the holding cell, she was forced to endure taunts.

As I sit here, Lee Roberts keeps coming by with various women. They stand there in their tight pink slacks and stare in. Lee usually makes a remark like "Can you believe it?" or "She's sure got big feet, hasn't she?"

Men have come by here and called me a "n----r fucker," a "bitch" etc. which has only brought giggles and laughter from members of the fair sex. Two girls came by. One asked . . . "Why do you run around with n-----s?" I replied that I didn't run around like she thought—that I only believed they should be treated like me. The other girl said, "Oh yeah, well why did God make them inferior and why did He make them slaves then?" I told her that God didn't make them slaves; men made them slaves. . . . It makes me uneasy, to say the least, to have people peering in and staring at me like an animal all day, especially when the obscenities start flying.

Judy was afraid but still managed to muster the composure needed to reflect on her experience.

I have been thinking a lot about the people who come by my cell. . . . Their accusations and remarks are so far removed from the real issue. . . . I believe the reason for their inability to discuss the real problem—that of one man's right to have as much of a chance as another man—is because they are so defensive.

I don't believe that they would be so defensive if they could admit their own mistakes and make their own effort to correct them. *But, since the North won the Civil War, they have always*

been in the position of having to defend what they know is wrong
[emphasis added].

Reading this portion of Judy's letter, Luke was reminded of what fifteen-year-old Loreace had written in her Freedom School essay about nonviolence: "Some whites think they are really, I mean, really hurting us, but in the eyes of God they are only hurting themselves."

Judy, Frank, and the others were released from jail the next day. Judy found that she had fared well in comparison, despite the taunts. Toward the end of the letter, she remarked, "All the men were beaten. Bozo's shirt was so torn it was practically falling off him. . . . There is a chance that we may sue individual policemen, namely Lee Roberts, for 'Assault and Battery' or something like that."

In this letter, Judy expressed a perception that was taking hold among activists in the civil rights movement. She concluded, "I certainly don't believe that the Negro should wait for the Southern White to work out his own problems before trying to get his rights." Everywhere, patience was wearing thin.

Following the letdown of Atlantic City, many African Americans lost trust in liberal whites, who were seen as having played a political game at the expense of the righteous moral cause of civil rights. This created divisions over strategy, especially within SNCC, the youthful organization at the forefront of Mississippi Freedom Summer.

Bubbling up from the turbulence, many raw questions surfaced. Nonviolence was being questioned. Black nationalism was emerging as a central issue. Black civil rights workers from the North, most of whom had joined the movement more recently than their southern brethren, were feeling the need to discover and define their Black identity. Looking back to this time, John Lewis wrote in his memoir, referring to "salt-of-the earth Southern black men and women": "In terms of black consciousness or black identity, they saw less need to take on the trappings of Africa, or to assert their blackness through things such as clothing and appearance. They didn't feel the same need to discover and assert their black identity, I guess, because they had never lost it in the first place."

✦ ✦ ✦

Adding to the general angst, as psychologist Robert Coles observed, most COFO volunteers and staff—both Black and white—were suffering from battle fatigue. Some people turned inward, while others acted out in anger.

Amid this, on February 21, militant, charismatic Malcolm X was assassinated. Revered by many, he had lately become more tolerant of whites after a pilgrimage to the Middle East. And then, just three days after Malcolm X's death, US District Judge William Harold Cox in Jackson, Mississippi, threw out all but two of the indictments John Doar had secured against the murderers just over a month ago. Among the nineteen Neshoba County conspirators, Sheriff Rainey and Deputy Sheriff Cecil Price were the only two who remained under indictment. Judge Cox was well known to be a diehard segregationist. Alas, in Mississippi, even in a federal court, nothing concerning justice was straightforward.

In her next letter to Luke, Judy reported: "After we heard of Judge Cox's Klan-like decision, we had a picket line in front of the federal building. . . . The line went for two days and was led by various members of the Chaney family. Some of the signs were 'Impeach Judge Cox' and 'Is Murder a Misdemeanor in Mississippi?'" Despite Judge Cox's decision, John Doar was not ready to give up or accept defeat. He appealed the case, hoping that a higher court would reverse Cox's decision. That, of course, would take time and demand both his persistence and patience over many years to come.

Judy included disturbing news about Bettye.

Bettye is all settled in Newton but is not very happy. The family she is with is just too middle class for her—she doesn't understand all this stress on togetherness. . . . However, the woman is extremely nice, and I'm sure she is willing to make a lot of compromises. . . . I guess I should have realized that these problems would arise with this family—but I felt so rushed to find her a place to stay, and this particular family was so excited about having her, and seemed so warm, that I got sold on it. I guess part of the problem that Bettye has is just plain being away from the movement.

✦ ✦ ✦

In early March, the civil rights movement was again center stage in the national news. Police and mounted deputies attacked nonviolent marchers led by Martin Luther King Jr. as they were attempting to cross the Edmund Pettus Bridge in Selma, Alabama. The atrocity, known as Bloody Sunday, was captured graphically in photos and TV footage broadcast across the country. Activists and supporters of the civil rights movement were outraged. The event only fueled their commitment to further resist.

In Rhode Island, Dad and Mom paid attention to these events in the news. They felt calmer now that Luke was back in Palo Alto, and thus they presumed he was safer.

For my part, I was again wrapped up in my college studies. My favorite course during the second semester was On Totalitarianism. Studying about Nazism and Stalinism wasn't everyone's cup of tea, and it certainly was depressing, but it felt weighty and important—posing essential questions about society and the dangers of authoritarianism. Al had finished all his coursework and looked forward to graduating in June. Some evenings, I sat in on an adult education history course he was teaching. At this time, Luke and I weren't in touch with each other. I assumed he was readjusting to life as a medical student at Stanford.

Chapter 26

SEGREGATION UP NORTH AND LESSONS LEARNED

At medical school, Luke needed to find outlets for his activism to maintain a sense of balance in his life. He rented a house in East Palo Alto. The community was integrated, and he enjoyed getting to know his neighbors. It wasn't long before he realized that the community lacked resources and political rights in many ways reminiscent of Mississippi. He could see that discriminatory effects of segregation also existed there. For example, it was obvious that neighboring Palo Alto—where Stanford was located—was extremely wealthy, pristine, and white. Integrated East Palo Alto, in contrast, was poor. Schools and other services suffered accordingly.

In the South, segregation was out in the open and enforced under Jim Crow laws. This southern system was called "*de jure* segregation"—segregation enshrined into law. However, redlining, and other widespread practices, created structural inequities—"*de facto* segregation"—not covered by laws. "De facto segregation" was prevalent throughout the North.

Back in July, President Johnson had signed the Civil Rights Act of 1964. Intentionally, it overturned *laws* but did nothing to address the *customs* of informal discrimination that were practiced nationwide. President Johnson and the Democratic leaders in Congress wanted to be sure that liberal northern legislators would vote yes to pass the bill. They understood that cutting too close to home—endangering customary practices that led to segregation—would be asking too much. Doing so would cost them precious votes. Thus, everywhere across the country, North and South, de facto segregation has continued to this day. It is a dominant, if unspoken, feature—a pillar supporting white privilege—that leaves a gaping hole in the national quest for equal rights.

Luke and his neighbors may not have been aware of the full picture, but they were very troubled by the consequences that they could easily see all around them. Getting acquainted with his neighbors, Luke learned there was an additional problem. East Palo Alto was an "unincorporated community" run by the San Mateo County Board. Because East Palo Alto lacked a municipal government, residents had no elected representatives of their own. To gain rights and a voice in their own affairs, a group of activists was strategizing how to take political action to incorporate the community. They were banding together with residents in other neighborhoods who had similar concerns. Luke discovered that some of his neighbors were also members of SNCC. Thus, he found an opportunity to return to community organizing right at his doorstep.

The group developed a plan of action and went door-to-door canvassing. The activists were optimistic, especially when the San Mateo County Board of Supervisors agreed to hold a referendum where citizens could vote on whether to incorporate. The county board was shocked when the activists' side won. But committed to keeping the status quo, they discounted the election results. Nevertheless, activists had prepared the groundwork for a campaign that would finally be successful in the distant future.

In whatever Luke was doing, nonviolence continued to be his touchstone. And despite any doubts he might have had, he remained true to what he'd learned during the Freedom Summer orientation. At the time he had written: "... it isn't easy to be nonviolent, but we feel that the means will determine the ends.

We are fighting a revolution and rather than using guns, we are fighting nonviolently through demonstrations." He participated in antinuclear protests. He volunteered to teach nonviolence after hours at the local public high school in East Palo Alto and at Pacifica High School, a private school in an affluent neighborhood. He sometimes held workshops on nonviolence for local teens at his home.

◆ ◆ ◆

By April, in Meridian, Judy's husband, Frank, wrote despondently to Luke, "The whole project is floundering." SNCC and CORE were no longer providing robust support. Many African American staff members were increasingly disturbed by the continued prominence and presence of white volunteers. Black staff felt it was time for the white activists to return home and deal with racism within their own communities. They felt this was most important since racism originates and comes out of the white community. White supremacy is maintained by institutions and customs of the white-power structure, as well as by discrimination by individuals and the silence of those who say they oppose racism but stand on the sidelines. This issue was at the forefront of discussions becoming ever more contentious.

Frank continued: "People don't know what to do about the Meridian movement, so we have turned inward for our existence: meaningless, busywork . . . the good kids have gone North. RETURN: a vacuum needs you."

Digesting this difficult news, Luke mulled over the consequences of what they had accomplished by testing the Civil Rights Bill in November. Poignantly, he wrote in his diary:

Eight students were arrested with us on that terrible night at the Toddle House Diner. All 8 were expelled from Harris High School. In order to graduate, most of them came North.

Bettye Manual went to Boston and is doing well in . . . school [but] she missed the freedom and independence of life in Meridian.

Willie Clark moved to NY. . . . He was so far behind in school that he couldn't make it and dropped out of the NY High School. He was so lonesome that he ran up an $800 phone bill calling Meridian.

The Waterhouses moved to Washington, and their family was broken up and the children distributed between two white families. They miss Mississippi and are not happy living in a white world.

The effect of our arrest was not to rally the Negro Community behind us. On the contrary, they were frightened and intimidated. They prevented their children from coming to Freedom School and Freedom School folded.

The bravest young student leaders went North. . . .

Despite these setbacks, Luke was optimistic about the prospect of long-term outcomes.

The price of Freedom is high. The results of our testing experience are difficult to evaluate, but I feel that this was a necessary step on the road to Freedom.

I feel that the most important contribution of our Freedom School was the training of future leaders for the Negro Community, leaders who will fight for their civil rights. And I feel that it was a valuable experience for teachers and students to meet and become friends. We met many of the students before they had learned to fear and hate white people.

And he proclaimed, "This is a proud time to be a Negro in America."

✦ ✦ ✦

Of course, Luke's medical studies and clinical rotations demanded most of his time and attention. Unlike most other medical schools, the program at Stanford was five years in length, which was intended to allow time for research. Now Luke had to decide on a medical specialty. Not surprisingly, given his formative experiences teaching in Meridian, Luke chose adolescent and child psychiatry with an emphasis on social psychology. This focus provided him with further insight into an omnipresent shadow that was deepening over the land and beyond: the war in Vietnam.

Chapter 27

ON VIOLENCE AND HATE, OF LOVE AND FREEDOM

By now, US involvement in the Vietnam War was rapidly escalating. In early March 1965, President Johnson launched a massive bombing campaign and ordered thirty-five hundred US Marines into Vietnam for the first time. Up until then, US soldiers had served only as military advisors. The number of combat ground troops sent to Vietnam kept increasing, and young men in the US, who had not voluntarily enlisted in the military, were facing the draft.

By mid-April, a thousand tons of bombs were dropped on the Vietcong, and soon afterward, fifteen thousand students gathered in Washington, DC, to protest the bombing campaign. Demonstrations against the war had started small but were now gaining national attention. In response, Luke wrote an unpublished essay titled "The Violent American." In it, he mused:

> If Sheriff Rainey had killed three boys in Vietnam, he would have been a national hero. Violence in the south is a symptom of the sickness in America.
>
> It is painful to acknowledge our violence. . . . We rationalize and bury our violence in words. Segregationists talk about God and the Constitution when they burn churches and deny the right to vote.

When we think of violence in America, we like to point to the South. . . . [But] we are all responsible.

The shadow of Vietnam was penetrating everywhere. A popular poster that hung in many dorm rooms at traditionally Black colleges quoted boxer and heavyweight champion Muhammad Ali, who famously refused to be drafted. He declared, "No Vietnamese ever called me n----r."

Frank confided in his letter to Luke from Meridian: "Unofficial news: Joe [Morse] has left for a brawl with the army; he is planning to go to jail rather than be inducted."

Drawing upon his renewed interest in psychology, Luke pondered the internal wellsprings of prejudice and violence.

Projection is the basis for all of our prejudices. We don't really hate Negroes or Communists. We don't really know them. They are scapegoats—Bad Guys, people whom everyone hates, people who are too weak to fight back.

We see them as symbols, and they represent the frustration, loneliness, and ugliness of our lives. We hate ourselves and we turn our anger on the scapegoats.

Luke's analysis echoed lessons I was learning in my class On Totalitarianism.

Scapegoats were easy to target because they were vulnerable and were, most likely, unable to fight back effectively. This had been true of the Jews under the Nazis and of the peasants under Stalin. It had been true, certainly, of slaves captured from Africa and carried against their will to American shores. And historically, for Blacks at a later time, it was true under the Jim Crow regime of white supremacy, which fed into the national nightmare from which we have yet to awaken.

Luke wondered, *Why have we humans harbored this tendency to demonize others?*

We are apathetic because we suppress our feelings and consider it "immature" to talk about love and hate.

 . . . It is realistic to be frightened.

 . . . It is imperative that we recognize and deal with our violence before we succumb to it.

These words of Luke's are worth repeating, like the lesson he taught his Freedom School students showing them that racism is based on a myth "less than skin deep." How much longer will we continue, Luke asked, to consider it immature to talk about love and hate?

✦ ✦ ✦

In April, at the same time Luke was writing his essay about Vietnam, Al received a letter he was eagerly awaiting from Harvard. In May, he would be graduating from Rochester with an undergraduate degree in English literature. The admissions committee not only accepted him into graduate school to study intellectual history but also awarded him a five-year fellowship. The fellowship promised to cover tuition costs, plus it included an extra stipend for living expenses and a year to do research abroad.

Naively, I agreed to follow him to Cambridge. I would need to apply as a transfer student to a college in the vicinity. Professor Sidney Monas, who taught the course On Totalitarianism, was shocked when he heard about my plans. He asked if I'd be willing to meet with him in his office.

He tried valiantly to dissuade me. "Julie, you can stay here and travel to see each other. Long distance relationships are possible, you know."

But I was too much the young romantic to listen to his cautionary words. My parents went along with my decision and never voiced any doubts. They were giving me the independence I thought I wanted.

✦ ✦ ✦

Judy wrote Luke a letter explaining that Frank had decided to apply to law school, and they were planning to leave Meridian. She reported that Joe Morse had been fortunate to gain conscientious-objector status and therefore would not need to dodge the draft. Gail was busy with her studies back at Radcliffe College.

In May, the *New Republic* magazine published an article Luke wrote, called "My Friends in Mississippi." In it, he recounted some of his experiences and what he'd learned as a volunteer during Freedom Summer. He wrote in detail about the children—5th Street Red, Lenray, and Ed, among others.

While Luke was in the process of writing these essays and articles, he was also compiling a scrapbook. He was thinking hard about the meaning of his Mississippi sojourn. *Could it possibly point to a way out? And if so, how?*

Luke reread an entry he'd made in his diary during the summer:

> It is tragic that barriers so foolish as color differences prevent whites and Negroes from knowing and loving each other—and it is only when these barriers are destroyed that any of us can find freedom.
>
> What the Negroes want is equality and after a lot of living together, individual Negroes and whites will be able to decide the question of love or hate on the basis of mutual understanding.

Had a foundation been laid for such "mutual understanding" during the hard work of Freedom Summer? Perhaps.

Luke's fellow volunteers were as busy as he was pondering the meaning of freedom in light of their experiences in Mississippi. Gail Falk wrote:

> These children will not grow up like their parents. Freedom songs have been their nursery rhymes. . . . For their parents "Freedom" still means danger and bombings and beatings.

For the children we knew, "Freedom" is beginning to mean friends and new ideas and being brave enough to start to dream about and choose the life they want to lead when they grow up and learning to make these dreams come true.

They are already, as one of the Freedom School students said, "free in the mind." And is this not a lot closer to the meaning of that word which none of us really understands?

✦ ✦ ✦

Music, in many ways, was at the heart of this beckoning but fragile opening toward social change. Judy Wright wrote about it in her notes.

> In a letter from my friend Luke, he told me that on the day of James Chaney's funeral in Meridian . . . as people wound their way down streets from all corners of the city to join in the peaceful march to the church, the words to We Shall Overcome rang out everywhere. It was a promise to James that his work would continue.
>
> I believe that the music of the movement enabled us to maintain the nonviolent stance that helped us reach our goals. It was easier not to fight back and to preserve our dignity when we were as one with others in deeply felt song.

Gail concurred. Soon after she'd left Mississippi to return to college in Cambridge, Massachusetts, Gail won the First Brotherhood Award of the *Pittsburgh Courier*. Published weekly, the *Pittsburgh Courier* was one of the leading African American newspapers in the United States. Pittsburgh was Gail's hometown. In February, Gail had sent her acceptance speech to her mother who was to read it. In it, she stated:

There is a verse to the song "We Shall Overcome" which goes: "We shall brothers be / We shall brothers be / We shall brothers be some day. / Deep in my heart I do believe / We shall overcome some day."

Sometimes that verse is followed by a verse "Black and White Together" and "We'll walk hand in hand. . . ."

Those verses were very beautiful to me in Mississippi, not so much because of off-in-the-future-some-day part of the dream but because they reminded me to look around the room where I was standing—standing as part of a circle—hand in hand with the person either side of me. "*Some day*," we sang in the song, but night after night meeting after meeting we were—as we sang—brothers, black and white together, standing hand in hand.

Hand in hand, their bodies swaying back and forth, in tune with each other and synched in rhythm, they lifted their voices and sang out as one. This was the "beloved community" at its best—nonviolent, committed to making a difference, and bonded together by song.

Chapter 28

CROSSING THE THRESHOLD

Luke was absorbed in his private life in other ways besides activism. Soon after he returned from Mississippi, a group of friends noticed him standing at the cashier's counter in the cafeteria.

"Look who's back!" exclaimed one, eagerly waving her arms to grab his attention.

Luke nonchalantly strolled over. Approaching the table, he spied a new face in the middle of the group. His friends pummeled him with questions about his time in Mississippi. As he answered between bites, he kept stealing glances her way. Afterward, he learned that she had taken a leave from her job on the East Coast as a speech therapist in a school. She had come to Stanford to take advanced classes. Luke was smitten.

He began to phone her repeatedly, but her roommate answered the phone, each time repeating, "Sorry. She's not here. She's out."

Her roommate became exasperated. "Syrtiller, look, you have no choice. You have to call him! *He's asking for you, but he's driving me crazy!*"

In the following months, Luke pursued Syrtiller McCollum relentlessly, sure as he was of his passion. She was more hesitant but did not resist. This was her first love affair, so, to her, it felt strange and new. Luke, meanwhile, kept it a secret tucked out of sight. He breathed not a word to our family. Only his peers at Stanford knew. Throughout the spring, Syrtiller clung to her original plan and had every intention of returning to the school where she worked in Wayne, New Jersey. Before she knew it, however, Luke was proposing marriage of all things and acting as if it were a *fait accompli*! Syrtiller did not resist.

Just one week before they were to marry, Luke finally called home to Rhode Island with the news. Their wedding would take place in Palo Alto. I was home from college for the summer. Al and I had taken up residence in the cabin down the hill.

Mom and Dad, being permissive parents, were especially so with me. I was the youngest of four, and we were now midway through the transformative decade of the 1960s. They also may have just been exhausted from previous rounds played out with my brothers, who were expected to hide their sexual liaisons. During their college years, both Luke and David had made it a habit to sneak up the hill from the cabin early in the mornings. I thought it was funny because we could so easily spy them slinking past the kitchen window on their way to their bedrooms in the wing off the side of the house. In contrast, Al and I were allowed to be open about the nature of our relationship.

In Luke's case, when it came to his love life, Mom had always stood like a stern guard at the gate. This time was no different except for her additional worry that his life would be more difficult now because Syrtiller was Black. Bubbe was more accepting and, like me, always trusted Luke's judgment sight unseen. Dad too had no qualms.

Syrtiller's parents and her two younger brothers would not make it out for the wedding. Luke talked to them over the phone. Her mother confided in Syrtiller that she approved of Luke's gentle, soft-spoken manner. From a distance she helped Syrtiller make all the wedding plans.

Luke was surprised that Syrtiller's brothers didn't try harder to test him or throw up obstacles.

"It was smooth sailing," he reported with relief. "They let me off easy."

Syrtiller stood up tall. "My parents taught my brothers a long time ago that because I'm the eldest they better show me respect and trust my judgment." She smiled, nodding. "They learned well."

Mom, Dad, and I packed in a flurry. Bubbe stayed behind at home and Al too. I was full of anticipation. I hadn't returned to California since we'd moved away when I was nine years old. I looked forward to meeting Luke's close friends and especially Syrtiller. I flew west with Mom and Dad wondering, *Who is she? What's she like?*

Luke met us at the airport, grinning. I practically leapt into his open arms. We tumbled into his old jalopy. He explained how one door, lopsided and almost hanging off, had to be closed carefully and tied with a rope. As he drove, I hung my head out the open window, relishing the warm California breeze and admiring the palm trees with odd curving trunks that lined the roadside. Mom and Dad were plying Luke nonstop with questions, but no one was listening for answers since everyone was chattering at once.

Approaching East Palo Alto, the homes shrank in size. To me, the neighborhood looked unassuming and cozy. Luke parked on the street in front of a low white picket fence, a small white house tucked behind it. Syrtiller greeted us with a crisp and lovely lilting voice. She had an engaging smile. I thought she was unusual looking with beautiful high cheekbones.

His fellow medical students trekked in and out of the house. These were the friends Luke had talked about for years. There was Joe Campbell who wanted not only to practice emergency medicine but also to open a winery. Irv Weissman was studious and sincere. He was planning to specialize in immunology and research. I thought Irv seemed familiar, like a Jewish uncle. Art Zelman had received Luke's letters from Mississippi and passed them on to be typed by a secretary. He came by with his wife, Virginia. The house was filled with their boisterous voices and laughter.

On the morning of their wedding, Luke asked if I'd like to come along. He was making a house visit to a sick child he'd treated recently at a clinic. He was doing this follow-up on his own, not because anyone had told him to. He parked the car in front of a modest house painted light green. The family greeted us warmly at the door and led us into the kitchen.

"The doctor's here to see you," the father called to his daughter. "Come!"

She entered the room, looking up at us shyly. About five years old, she was very skinny. Luke lifted her up so she could sit on the table. He examined her under the one hanging, bare lightbulb. As a premed student, I was planning to follow in my brother's footsteps. I carefully observed the tender manner of his touch and his gentle voice, how he treated this young girl and her family with humility and respect. I was disturbed by the poverty so evident in their home and furnishings but moved by her parents' affection and concern.

In the late afternoon, Luke needed to drive to the airport to pick up our brother, David, and his wife, Sue. Again, he asked if I wanted to come along. We left late and traffic was dense, so we were running late.

"Hey, you know you could be late to your own wedding!" I chided.

"Yeah, but they'll have to wait for me, won't they?"

Luke parked the car in the lot, and as was my habit from childhood, I challenged him. "*Let's race!*"

I took off before he could reply, and he followed, but my heart skipped when I realized he wasn't winning. Luke had always won.

He was winded and seemed to be having trouble keeping up. I slowed down, and we walked. *Something's wrong*, I thought but quickly tucked it away. We were in a hurry and excited to see David and Sue.

The four of us piled back into the car and dashed off to the wedding. We arrived without a moment to spare at the Palo Alto

Wedding photo of Luke and Syrtiller, July 16, 1965. Courtesy of Syrtiller Kabat.

Unitarian Church. Our sister, Alix, had come from Berkeley, so we three siblings were present—David, Alix, and me—plus Sue. The Unitarian minister Dan Lion was a good friend and, like Luke, a devoted student and teacher of nonviolence.

Afterward, close friends and family gathered for a simple reception at their home. Music blared. Folks danced in the living room by the picture window or chatted over food and drinks in the kitchen. After a few hours, I left with Mom and Dad, but Luke, Syrtiller, and their friends danced into the wee hours of the night.

The next day, Luke boasted that while dancing and spinning a particularly large friend of his from medical school, he enthusiastically lifted her into the air before realizing what he was doing, not

Wedding hug (Luke, Julie, Syrtiller). Courtesy of Syrtiller Kabat.

only surprising her but also delighting himself. Luke looked tired and deeply contented. Now entering his last year of medical school, he would graduate next June. His future with Syrtiller looked bright.

✦ ✦ ✦

Returning home, I turned my attention to preparing for my own wedding, scheduled for August 1, less than two weeks away. Everything seemed to be moving too fast, and I was confused, but I tried hard not to show it. Having lost touch with my old high school friends, I had no one my own age to confide in. *What am I doing?* I asked myself. Honestly, I had no idea.

About one month prior, back in June at age eighteen, I had agreed to marry Al Schwartz. Little did I know that, behind the scenes, Al's mother had been pressuring him to marry me. More conventional than my parents, she was offended. She believed it was improper for us to live together unwed. Al never mentioned this to me; his mother's pressure was a secret he kept tucked away. And he never formally proposed. Rather, once we moved into the cabin, he kept floating the idea of marriage.

"Let's get married," he'd say.

Each time I'd reply, "No. I'm not ready, I'm too young."

Despite my steady answer, Al didn't relent. And he wouldn't take no for an answer.

In addition to feeling pressured behind the scenes by his mother, Al was caught in a cycle of sibling rivalry with his identical twin brother, Murray. Murray had married Peggy the year before.

Eventually, I succumbed, inwardly asking myself, *Really, what's the difference?* As I was immature and unworldly, I reasoned that I love him. So, *Why not?*

Luke and David reacted to the news by taking opposite sides. Luke, as always, trusted my judgment sight unseen. David was already married to Sue. Their wedding had taken place just after they'd both graduated from college three years ago.

He phoned to warn me, "You're marrying too young. Don't do it."

Young and headstrong, I plowed ahead.

A rabbi from Providence would conduct the wedding ceremony. His wife was a good friend of Mom's. Al and I met him in advance to prepare for the ceremony.

He turned and gazed down at me rather sternly. "You realize, of course, that you and your family want the fruits [of Judaism] without the roots."

I winced.

Luke and Syrtiller did not make it out for our wedding, but David came with Sue, and Alix came too. Al and I were married outdoors under a jerry-rigged chuppah beside the house, overlooking the

Narragansett Bay. My friend from a Lebanese family provided the music. He had taught me music lessons on the oud, the Arabic version of a lute. An older man accompanied him on the *doumbek*, an hourglass-shaped Middle Eastern drum. Thus, we had Arabic music at our Jewish wedding. They also played the traditional Israeli *hora*, so we could dance. To me, the music represented a fitting American mix of cultures. *If only it could be like this*—blending cultures peacefully—*in the whole wide world*, I thought.

For a honeymoon, Al and I drove across country to visit family. Some nights we camped out in the open under the stars. Enroute, on August 6, President Johnson signed the Voting Rights Act of 1965. It outlawed state and local practices that prevented Blacks from voting. Literacy tests, poll taxes, and other forms of intimidation were now banned. Importantly, the law included safeguards. The fiery words of Fannie Lou Hamer and the actions by the Mississippi Freedom Democratic Party at the national convention had had an impact. This law represented the high point and the legal triumph of the civil rights movement. Although we were not in touch with Luke, Al and I knew he and his activist friends would be celebrating too—no doubt about it.

Al and I stayed in Berkeley at the home of his twin brother, Murray, and his wife, Peggy. During our stay, I saw my sister Alix, and we visited Luke and Syrtiller in East Palo Alto. Luke filled in some of the blanks about his time in Meridian. In jail, he said, he had attended to a sick prisoner. He explained that he could never forgo helping someone as a doctor no matter how repelled he might be by their racism or other views.

✦ ✦ ✦

In the fall, Luke and Syrtiller settled into their married life in East Palo Alto. They went together to antiwar and antinuclear protests. They demonstrated in support of the California grape pickers' strike led by Cesar Chavez and Dolores Huerta. They traveled to

Delano, at the center of the strike, where they met Chavez. Closer to home, they continued working with activists on the goal of incorporating East Palo Alto. Luke began meeting with a small group to plan a summer Freedom School for teens, modeled on the Meridian Freedom School. He dreamed of opening a free medical-dental community clinic in East Palo Alto. This project, close to his heart, would combine knowledge of medicine and community service.

Al and I moved into a tiny three-room apartment within easy walking distance of Harvard Square. The apartment, painted a dull rose-colored beige, was drab and unappealing but convenient. Al claimed the bedroom as his study. The living room served as our bedroom and my study, plus a good-sized but bare-bones kitchen.

I was unprepared for my new role as wife. Being traditional and given the times, Al assumed I would take care of all the housework and practical matters. Little did I know that in the years to come this would sprout, for me, into staunch feminism.

Al began graduate studies. I commuted across the Charles River to Boston University by bike whenever possible, otherwise by public transportation. With little time to spare between school and housework, I made no friends of my own except for the downstairs neighbors, Bill, Barbara, and their delightful six-month-old baby boy. Al's fellow graduate students came around. Ironically, the young men consulted me, in all seriousness, about their relationships with women. Considerably older, they looked upon me as the wise married woman. How silly! I knew that but nevertheless took the bait.

✦ ✦ ✦

In December, Luke and Syrtiller journeyed east for the holidays to visit our family and hers. They came to see Al and me. Wandering by the Charles River and around the city, we chattered nonstop. It was approaching evening when Luke announced that he and Syrtiller wanted to stay overnight. Al and I were totally unprepared. All we had to offer them was a dilapidated padded armchair in Al's study.

Luke was emphatic. "Don't worry! It's fine. This will work for us."

When they were alone, he sat and gestured Syrtiller to sit on his lap.

"Luke . . . I'll be a dead weight once I'm asleep."

"Shh . . ." he reassured her. "It's alright."

Luke held her on his lap through the night. Covered only by a thin blanket in the drafty room, Syrtiller was convinced she'd freeze to death. In the morning, too considerate, neither one of them uttered a word of complaint.

By noon, they departed and went on to visit Bettye Manual, Luke's Meridian Freedom School student expelled from Harris High. Bettye and Luke were thrilled to see each other, but she told them she was not having an easy time.

For my part, I began to miss Luke as soon as they left. We hadn't made any concrete plans to see each other again.

Luke and Syrtiller briefly returned to Rhode Island on their way to visit Syrtiller's family on the South Jersey shore, just across from Atlantic City. Luke met her parents and two brothers. Syrtiller's father owned a construction company that made custom-made homes. Her mother regaled Luke with stories. He was especially captivated by a tale enshrined in their family lore. Syrtiller's great-great-grandmother, born a slave, had escaped by the Underground Railroad. Reaching Canada and freedom, she decided to rename herself to claim her own identity. She chose the name she thought was most beautiful of all: Syrtiller. Luke winked at Syrtiller, wiser now.

Her parents and brothers approved of Luke. Being Jewish, he felt a sense of triumph being so well accepted.

"He's a loving, kind, and respectful man," her mother told Syrtiller in confidence. But she continued, "Why aren't you wearing stockings? What's happened to your proper sense of style? He mustn't interfere!"

It's really not a big deal, Syrtiller thought to herself, but her mother disagreed.

✦ ✦ ✦

After the flurry of holiday visits, the four of us settled into our respective routines on opposite coasts. Luke applied to academic teaching hospitals, went for interviews, and was matched with the Menninger Clinic's School of Psychiatry at the University of Kansas in Missouri. He looked forward to his internship and residency. Syrtiller was teaching at San Jose State University and practicing as a speech therapist. Luke was attempting to get her to quit and be his full-time wife, but she was unconvinced.

"Where in the world will the money come from, for me to do that?!"

Like most men at the time, Luke was old-fashioned when it came to thinking about women's roles and a woman's place in the world.

Meanwhile, the East Palo Alto activist group received good news. They received a grant to hire a community organizer. They chose Bob Hoover, one of the original organizers who was devoted to the mission. Bob convinced many churches and other organizations to come together to support the cause. He spearheaded planning for a multifaceted campaign. It included running candidates for the local school board and offering a summer Freedom School.

✦ ✦ ✦

In mid-April, Luke phoned home. "I think you ought to know, Mom, that I'm in the hospital. It seems to be pneumonia."

Less than a week later, on April 25, after having an X-ray, he entered a small room where several doctors were closely examining a large chest X-ray up on the screen.

Luke walked over to join them.

"Oh dear," he remarked. "That person doesn't have long to live."

A doctor turned toward him. "Dr. Kabat," he said gently, "please have a seat." Taking a breath, he paused a moment.

"Those are your lungs."

✦ ✦ ✦

At the time, when Luke phoned Mom and Dad with his news, Al and I were on the highway driving to Rhode Island. We knew Luke was ill, but that was all. When we walked up to the house and opened the door, I heard Mom screaming. My heart raced as I bounded upstairs.

In the bedroom, she was lying on her belly, furiously punching and kicking the bed, and repeating between sobs:

"It's cancer. Oh my God, it's cancer."

✦ ✦ ✦

That evening, without delay, David flew up from Southern California to see Luke.

Mom flew out the next morning, and Dad and I, the day after. Only our sister Alix was unaware. She was far away in Paris, France, taking courses at the Sorbonne, accompanying her new husband, Lee, who was on a fellowship to study music composition.

The morning Dad and I arrived, Luke was at the hospital for a procedure. I waited anxiously on the couch, peering out the picture window. Luke emerged from the car and my heart dropped. Bent over and weak, in a flash, he'd become drawn and thin. His lungs were filling with fluid, and he was finding it hard to breathe.

I moaned inside.

But as soon as he saw me and we hugged, he began joking to break the spell.

✦ ✦ ✦

During my week's stay, I slept in the extra room just off the kitchen, while other family members stayed at a nearby motel. I watched as Luke's close friends came and went, attentive and caring. Luke was gracious, listening and asking probing questions about their upcoming internships. There was plenty of laughter mixed in too, most often black humor.

He and I found a few precious occasions to talk alone. In one such conversation, he advised me not to go to medical school.

"Pig, do something else instead—where you'll have more time for yourself."

✦ ✦ ✦

As a young doctor, Luke understood the gravity of what was happening in his body. Syrtiller and I, in contrast, did not realize the full extent of the danger he faced. Since there were no current medical treatments available, he applied to be accepted into a clinical trial that his friend Irv Weissman had identified. In this way, Luke understood he would further the scientific research, with the outside chance he might find a miracle cure.

✦ ✦ ✦

Before leaving to take my final exams at college, I told them that I'd be back in June.

"Al and I will come out for the summer," I promised. "We'll find a place to stay nearby."

Dad and I flew back east together. Dad was struggling and in denial. He was holding out hope that the doctors were wrong about the diagnosis.

David, still in graduate school at Caltech, was living in Pasadena near Los Angeles. Being closer, he was able to come back and visit often. Mom planned to stay on indefinitely at the home of their friend Mary Beth. Syrtiller was constantly by Luke's side.

Luke and Syrtiller. Courtesy of Syrtiller Kabat.

There were moments of lightness in the days that followed. When Mom saw him one afternoon in the backyard, lying out in the sun, she asked, "Lucien, what can I do for you?"

"Oh—" He squinted up at the sun. After a pause, he smiled. "I'd like it if you'd read to me . . . *Zorba the Greek*. The dancing, my favorite—"

Mom scurried into the house, and it took her no time at all to find his dog-eared copy of the book by Nikos Kazantzakis.

In earlier times, all of us had seen Luke stop what he was doing sometimes, snap his fingers, begin to sway, and then hum and dance. Often, he'd recite a few lines from the book or the movie, which he knew by heart.

In the garden where he lay, neighborhood children were climbing the tree. They sat above him on the branches. Laughing, the children threw apples down for Luke to catch while Mom read to him.

That evening, Mom wrote in her diary: "Lucien has a belly laugh that's contagious. It gives anyone who's with him a sense of joy to be alive and in the company of so great and good a fellow-creature."

But the passing moments of lightness sprang from deepening shadows. Luke's last chapter was brief. The lung cancer was aggressive. He was accepted into a clinical trial that seemed promising, but he didn't receive any treatments. He died too soon—May 27, 1966, just two weeks after his twenty-seventh birthday and one month after the diagnosis.

✦ ✦ ✦

Dad immediately flew west. Al and I flew with him to La Guardia but waited there to meet Alix. She was flying in from Paris, and her plane arrived late that night. Alix believed she was on her way to California to visit Luke. I needed to inform her of the truth. The three of us boarded the next plane to California. Not having seen Luke ill and hardly having heard any news, Alix was in shock. She was finding it next to impossible to realize he was dead. Even though I had seen him ill—and had felt his spirit touch me with a shiver when he died, I too found it too much to grasp.

Luke's memorial service was held three days after he died. That morning, I visited the funeral home. Viewing the closed casket, I kept trying to convince myself that my brother's body was inside. The family was gathering. David and his wife, Sue, were already there, of course. Mom's beloved sister, our Aunt Angie, came, as did Uncle Sam, Dad's brother Jack, and their wives, in addition to cousins and friends.

The memorial service took place during the afternoon in Luke and Syrtiller's backyard. An informal affair, we sat on chairs in a circle sharing stories.

Stokely Carmichael came as the representative of SNCC and was first to speak. "Luke is a hero of the people," he began.

One man attended who had met Luke only once at a protest, but he talked about what a strong impression Luke had made on him. "I read about this in the newspaper. I had to be here."

Someone read a commemorative letter signed by Cesar Chavez and other members of the farm workers' strike.

At Luke's request, near the end of the service, I sang the Pete Seeger song he cherished, "Turn, Turn, Turn." Syrtiller told me that, during his illness, Luke listened to this song, playing the tape I'd made for him during Freedom Summer over and over again. Based on the Bible's Ecclesiastes, the song was a source of consolation for him. According to the Bible: "All things have their time . . . under heaven. . . . A time to be born and a time to die. A time to plant and a time to reap."

It was hard to sing through my tears.

Afterward, everyone rose. Folding our arms across our chests, we held hands. Swaying side to side, we sang to the world, the sun, and the stars, "We shall overcome. / We shall overcome someday."

✦ ✦ ✦

We shall overcome. Yes. Luke believed it.

But how?

How can we make the promise real?

✦ ✦ ✦

During Freedom Summer, Luke was often caught off guard, challenged as all the volunteers were, when he needed to respond quickly to new situations. When, for instance, was it wise *not* to act like the professional he was training to be? In a letter written after his very first week in Mississippi, Luke confided: "I gave 'medical' advice earlier this week to a father whose son had an abscess on his chest. I told him to take the kid to a doctor. The father thanked me and kissed my hand. I was embarrassed and didn't know what to do so I kissed his hand."

✦ ✦ ✦

We shall overcome: humility and respect point toward one pathway.

✦ ✦ ✦

Many years later, when Mom was at the Hospice Inn in Providence, grateful to be helped in her dying, an African American nurse stopped by to check on her. She bent down briefly to confer with her. When she stood up to leave, Mom quickly asked, "May I kiss your hand?"

Kindly, the nurse complied.

After she left the room, Mom glanced over at me and murmured, "Black, white—It's all so silly." Mom's deepening friendship with Syrtiller had helped her to see.

It was amazing grace.

✦ ✦ ✦

Friendship and love: *we shall overcome*.

✦ ✦ ✦

As a volunteer during Freedom Summer, Luke had grappled with the realities of nonviolence, both as a principle and as a tactic. Little did he know he was creating his own epitaph when one day he

Rough sketch of Luke's gravestone. From the author's collection of Sarah
Kabat's private papers.

scribbled into his diary: "I am fighting a nonviolent battle because I believe that hate begets hate and perhaps that love begets love."

"Perhaps," he had written. But our mother turned it into a resounding *yes!*

As she contemplated which words to choose for the epitaph on his gravestone, she decided to quote just the last three: "*Love begets love.*"

✦ ✦ ✦

Was she right to do so?

How *shall* we overcome?

It is a question worth asking. . . .

✦ ✦ ✦

I trust Luke would say it is up to us, the living, to find out. . . .

AFTERWORD

During his last month, Mom wrote in her diary that she told Luke she regretted the fact he had faced so many challenges in his short life. But Luke comforted her and replied, as she phrased it: "He had had the chance to live life vicariously all the stages of man, for in his medical education he brought children into the world by assisting at their birth, and as a doctor followed people in their vicissitudes and changing periods through the seven different decades of life described by the poets, thus coming to feel he had tasted all of life through his knowledge and growth." She added, "He never went the easy route alas."

When Luke had written his letter on a napkin before going to Mississippi, he had explained why he wanted to go:

> I intend to live a principled life and to work for the things I
> believe—This helps to give purpose to my life—
> . . . If you ask "why does he want to live an ideal?—what a child-
> ish thing—he's a *bissl mishuganeh* [a little bit crazy] etc." then I
> must say that I have observed the lives of a few people in Palo Alto
> who are living their ideals. They believe that failing to take a stand
> and rationalizing away your responsibility for what happens while
> you live will result in longevity if that happens to be your goal but
> also in failure to live in a real sense.

✦ ✦ ✦

Luke's remains traveled east by train for burial in Deep River, Connecticut. A close friend of Dad's, Hal Samuels, helped supervise the Jewish section of the cemetery there. In the blur of grief, Mom and Dad turned to him for advice. Luke's burial plot sat on a hill near woods overlooking the river. Only Bubbe, Mom, and Aunt Angie were present for the interment. Syrtiller, Dad, and I waited back at home in Rhode Island, searching through old family photos.

Later that day, I went home to Al who was waiting in Cambridge. Syrtiller left also. As soon as we departed, Mom and Dad returned privately to the new grave, offering prayers and planting yews.

✦ ✦ ✦

Everyone was overwhelmed by grief following Luke's untimely death. *Why lung cancer?* we wondered. He was never a smoker. He was so young and so needed in the world. It made no sense.

Syrtiller was not only dazed but also understandably angry. Her anger powered action and helped her put on a strong front. Shortly after returning home after the burial, she was present on June 14 for Stanford University School of Medicine's graduation ceremony. The next day, Dr. Robert Glaser, dean of the medical school, wrote her a heartfelt letter. "Thank you for being with us to receive Lucien's degree last Sunday. I am sure that it was a trying experience for you but at the same time it did provide us with an opportunity to express our affection and respect for Lucien, and I know all of his classmates particularly were gratified that you were willing to join us." Dr. Glaser enclosed a copy of the Honors Convocation program and remarks he'd made in honor of Luke, which began:

> Lucien Kabat was born on May 13, 1939, in Minneapolis, Minnesota, the son of Dr. and Mrs. Herman Kabat. He attended high school in El Cerrito, California, and after spending one year at Antioch College, he transferred to the University of Rhode

Island. . . . His academic achievements at Rhode Island led to his being named the outstanding pre-medical student in his class; while an undergraduate, he pursued original research in the field of immunology, and as well, found time to write for the school's literary magazine.

. . . Lucien was deeply involved in the civil rights movement, and in his fourth year, he spent some months in Mississippi as a volunteer worker with the Student Nonviolent Coordinating Committee in which he was keenly interested. He taught Biology and Public Health in a Freedom School.

Dr. Glaser concluded: "We mourn his loss and we shall ever honor his name on the rolls of the graduates of this School. . . . Lucien Kabat completed the requirements for the degree of Doctor of Medicine. Saddened though we are that he is not with us to receive his degree, I do want to present the diploma he so well deserved to his widow, Mrs. Kabat."

✦ ✦ ✦

For the next six years, Syrtiller dedicated herself to bringing Luke's visions and dreams to fruition.

"I was rather reserved before and preferred to organize behind the scenes," she said, "but in memory of Luke, I stepped out front."

She kept telling herself, his dreams can't die. She ran for and won a seat on the local school board, supported by Bob Hoover and his community organization, and she worked with others to make the East Palo Alto medical-dental clinic a reality. Under a different name, the Ravenswood Family Health Center, this clinic is still operating today.

"Because of Luke, I awoke and returned to visible activism," she has said.

After Luke died, Syrtiller dropped out of graduate school at Stanford but continued to teach at San Jose State University.

There, she began offering courses in death and dying and studied with Elisabeth Kubler Ross. Syrtiller entered a new graduate program, achieving a PhD with a double major in clinical and social psychology.

Within our family, Luke had held out a beacon of light. After his death, each one of us stepped into a long-lasting cocoon of grief. How could it be otherwise? The ways in which we adapted were different, of course.

My path through grief, like everyone else's, unfolded in stages that overlapped with each other and cycled back for another round. After singing at Luke's funeral, I stopped. I shut down. I transferred to Brandeis University and majored in philosophy, hoping to probe the meaning of life. The flood gates opened wide for me two years later when my first daughter, Tanya, was born. Holding this beloved infant close to my heart, I sang to her for hours, accompanied by the steady swish of the rocking chair. Speeding on a Los Angeles thruway about five years after Luke's death, I began to hum, and a short song took shape. "Oh, my brother / Beloved brother / I carry your song within me / Your laughter resides there too / I walk in the world strong / In thought of you."

✦ ✦ ✦

As a basic scientist, David set out to research cancer on the cellular level. This led him to study retroviruses as he inquired, How does the virus manage to invade a healthy cell? In memory of Luke, David sought scientific breakthroughs. On his own time, he also worked generously on behalf of refugees.

Mom and Alix each fell into a deep depression.

For Mom, it was the voice of her granddaughter, following five dark years, that rekindled her desire to embrace life.

Tanya called to her from the yard, "Come play school! I have the desk all ready. I'm gonna be the teacher, OK?"

Alix found solace by offering daycare to babies and young children in her home and caring for her own newborn sons.

Dad kept Luke's doctor bag with its stethoscope and other contents, carefully placed for safekeeping, on top of his bedroom bureau. He gazed at it every day. He developed a mantra he recited: "Do what you love. After all, you don't know how long you have."

After college, as I wrestled with deciding which career path to take, Dad repeated this frequently, sometimes adding, "I see you're playing the piano, not studying chemistry. I don't see you cracking that textbook. Follow your heart, Julie, do the music."

Before he died, Luke had also advised me *not* to become a doctor. "Do something else, where you have more time for yourself."

At the time, I was trying to review college chemistry to qualify for medical school. In the bookstore, when I'd stretched up to lift the heavy chemistry text off the shelf, a line of William Butler Yeats's ran unbidden through my mind: "Too long a sacrifice / Can make a stone of the heart. / O when may it suffice?"

Memories of Luke have been a guidepost for me through the years, as a single mother with my two daughters, in my friendships, and in my work. After ten years of marriage, Al and I had drifted irrevocably apart and divorced. Facing outward, I needed to rebuild my confidence and carve out my own path. For forty years, as a teaching artist and composer in residence in public schools, I aspired to help children open their imaginations and express their sense of wonder through the performing arts. Inviting them, like a benign Pied Piper, into an inquisitive space, I came to understand the joy Luke found in teaching.

✦ ✦ ✦

Luke's friends carried the feeling of his warmth and compassion into the world in a myriad of ways. Twenty-three years after Luke's death, in 1989, his close friend from medical school, Irv Weissman, wrote a letter to our parents:

Luke as a living memory often helps me when cynicism and greed and lack of commitment to human endeavors and liberties seem to be the overwhelming motivations of those around us. . . . When the tendency for me is to turn inward, Luke's memory helps me turn outward again. I'll never forget . . . one night at that house in East Palo Alto, Luke and I and Syrtiller . . . were talking, and Luke, sometimes short of breath, wondered if there were any dramatic gesture we could make to help America understand the enormous evil of that developing war [in Vietnam]. That was Luke, stuck in the middle of a losing battle for his life, knowing enough about medicine to know it was a losing battle, and still thinking of a way in which he could help people who would live after him.

✦ ✦ ✦

Luke's Freedom School students used what they had learned as they moved on to adulthood.

Dorothy reminisced about how Luke had taught her how to read aloud.

"He told me to slow down, slow down. I was stumbling 'cause I went too fast." She shrugged her shoulders and shook her head with amusement. "I just tried to go too fast."

Dorothy had many opportunities to practice in her thirty-two years as a daycare and Head Start teacher.

Andreesa became a health therapist and worked at the main psychiatric center in Albany. *Will Andreesa become a doctor?* Luke had wondered.

Lenray, the "dreamer kid," became a minister and works for the Navy. He is writing a book, *Freedom Fighters, in the Eyes of a Child.* We connected through conversation and email, and he reflected:

People thought we couldn't exist together.
    Luke is one of my heroes. . . . I truly loved Luke! All of us kids did. . . .

When we kids saw Luke or Freeman, we would forget all else and everyone else. We could feel their love and care for us. It was golden. It was magic. It was real.

Mickey, James, Andy, Rita . . . Sam, Patti, Mark, Gail, Free, Luke . . . our friends, our extended family . . . and others . . . inspired us . . . they were earth angels.

Luke would have been proud of the Meridian children he came to love.

No matter what they achieved outwardly, his measure of success would have been at one with Gail's Freedom School student, who had proclaimed during Freedom Summer that he was learning to be "free in the mind."

✦ ✦ ✦

Mississippi Freedom Summer was a brave and unique experiment in creating social change. Have things changed because of the summer and the larger 1960s civil rights movement of which it was a part?

Yes and no.

Tragically, bias and structural racism are baked into the bones of our American culture and history. This spawns a nightmare from which we must struggle to awaken.

But there are sometimes glints of light that dart through the darkness, to be found if one looks closely. A few years ago, I was working as a teaching artist with a first-grade class. Their public school in the small city of Hudson, New York, was very diverse.

The principal once said, "I love coming to school here because it's like the United Nations."

So that day, as on all days, the boys and the girls sitting around me in a circle on the floor revealed all shades of skin colors and were wearing many different, colorful styles of clothes. The topic of the workshop was why we celebrate Martin Luther King Day.

Luke and Ben Chaney. © 1976 David Prince/Take Stock/TopFoto.

The caption in *Mississippi Eyes* (2014) by Matt Herron reads: "Like any young man trying to deal with the loss of an older brother, who was both a mentor and a role model, Ben Chaney passed through periods of reflection and pain, as well as other moments when he simply forgot about his loss and was just a kid. In looking for someone to fill the void, he often turned to older civil rights workers such as Luke Kabat, who were close by."

I wanted to tell the children about Luke and share some of his story. We sang freedom songs while we marched around the classroom, their teacher Beth Barnes bringing up the rear. Singing and snaking our way around their desks, they eagerly added verses of their own, relevant to their world and their concerns. Seated back on the rug, I proudly held up a photo where Luke was tenderly looking down at his young friend Ben Chaney.

"Here's Luke," I said.

Before I could say more, one boy couldn't contain himself and blurted out a question without raising his hand. "Miss Julie, which one is your brother?"

Taken aback, I laughed with delight and could only wonder, *Would this have happened in 1964?*

TOWARD A MORE PERFECT UNION

In narrating Luke's story, I have touched on history and issues that arose at the time for him, his friends, other civil rights activists, and our family. Today, as I come to the end of writing this memoir, the United States faces trauma on all fronts. The COVID-19 pandemic is raging. The economy is in danger of collapse. African Americans are bringing to light continued and rampant racial injustice, and cell-phone videos capturing horrific police brutality abound. Voting rights are being eroded. Our most cherished democratic values and norms are in peril. In terms of health, safety, and economic impacts, African Americans are experiencing the greatest risk and the worst outcomes. This is no surprise given our history but nonetheless shocking. Outraged masses of people everywhere—not only across this nation but also abroad—are taking to the streets to protest racial injustice.

My sister-in-law Syrtiller reminds me, "What people of color want is very simple—and guaranteed by the Constitution—to be treated fairly. Whites treating others the way they would like to be treated. Either everyone is privileged, or no one is."

Yet, in the midst of this chaos and trauma, we can begin to glimpse a better future, one almost beyond imagining just a short time ago. Systemic changes are necessary.

At the same time, I believe that Luke would caution us to look inside as well as out. Thinking about the Vietnam War, he wrote, "It is imperative that we recognize and deal with our violence before we succumb to it."

White supremacy has always been and remains *violent* at its core. The violence exists on all levels—*within* each of us—affecting our relationships with one another and how we exist and act as a local community, society, nation, and as one nation among others on the international stage. That violence is eating away at each of us, including those who believe they are above the fray.

A true ending to the Civil War calls on us—all colors and cultures—to seek true reconciliation between the races. The end to a race-based nation demands no less. Somewhere, seeing we are picking up his dream, I know that Luke is smiling.

A STORY
BEHIND THE STORY

Years ago, I jotted down some of my early childhood memories of Luke to share with my grandchildren. When I read the first draft aloud to my partner, Wayne, he suggested that I rewrite it in the first-person present. This was a revelation. Writing as my child-self, a wondrous feeling emerged: *Luke is here.* As I continued writing, I began to understand more vividly how central Luke had been in inspiring and shaping the person I've become. I also realized how Luke's story of Freedom Summer might inspire others too.

At this point, the reader might wonder, *How did this story, this book, come to be?* To convey the sense of adventure I felt as my writing journey evolved, I have chosen to write the acknowledgements from a different vantage point.

In the present tense . . . we are . . . here . . . now.

Schiermonnikoog, Wadden Islands, the Netherlands

Summer sand and wind and a tiny beach house:

I'm visiting my daughter Rivke Van der Lugt, son-in-law Remko, and the grandchildren. My second daughter is named Rebecca, after our beloved Bubbe, but since immigrating to the Netherlands, she has changed her nickname from Becky to Rivke. This is what Bubbe was called as a young girl growing up in the Old Country.

"I feel closer to her this way," my daughter says.

This is not the first time we are spending our summer holiday together on this quaint island. I have a small bedroom in the rented family cottage. I am delighted, every time, to hear the children calling me. As a bit of a joke, and to distinguish myself, I have Americanized the spelling of my name. And so, to them, I am Bubby.

At night, I tuck my granddaughter Sarah into bed, eager to sing songs and make up stories to please her. But tonight, Sarah has other ideas—real stories are on her mind.

"Bubby, will you tell me stories from your childhood?"

I decide to think up funny stories to tell her, one each night. After two nights, Sarah's older brother, Sam, approaches.

"I hear you laughing away in there, Bubby. Can't you tell your stories to all of us?"

I share one story each night after dinner while we are sitting outdoors around the picnic table. I keep searching out the funny ones and regale them to rollicking laughter.

Years later, I attend a workshop on writing a memoir at our little rural library up the road. I've grown tired of writing grants that furnish the bread and butter for my career in music. I have no intention of writing a memoir, but perhaps this introduction will provide me with food for thought. Walking home, just for the fun of it, I wonder, *If I were to write a memoir what . . . ?* I think of the family stories I've told Sam and Sarah and how they've enjoyed learning about my childhood.

In a flash, I sense Luke's presence nearby and realize for the first time: as important as he was in shaping my passions and approach to life—and as courageous as his activism was for the cause of freedom—my grandchildren will never know him. Unless I *tell* them. These stories will be more complicated than the funny childhood stories I've shared so far. It will require writing . . . a memoir.

Growing up in the Netherlands, Sam and Sarah know very little about American history. These stories will provide them with some background. I begin scribbling early childhood stories into a checkerboard notebook that reminds me of school days. Looking ahead, I know I will want to write about Luke's experience as a volunteer during Freedom Summer. That will require research, but for now, this task is off in the future.

Portland, Oregon

A balmy spring breeze rustles leaves on the tree-lined street. I'm sitting at a round table on my brother's front porch, surrounded by papers and a stack of newly purchased folders. A wooden box with its familiar carved top lays open beside me.

Before coming, I had explained to my brother, David Kabat, and his wife, Virginia Greene, that I am planning to write about Luke. In the few days prior, David and I have been talking in depth, for the first time ever, about our beloved brother. David has shared memories from their early childhood—how protective Luke was and how much he wanted to explain things to teach David about the world.

On the phone beforehand, I said, "Let's visit first, but then I'd like to spend a few extra days working on my own and going through the box. OK?"

Years before, when David, Alix, and I had dismantled Mom and Dad's home, David had asked to have Mom's precious box of Luke's writings. She kept it in their bedroom. It took pride of place on Dad's bureau next to Luke's doctor bag.

David sighed. "It's still in the same brown packing paper as when it came. I opened it once. Mom's diary from Luke's dying was on top. I picked it up and started to read, but it was too painful. I put it back, closed the box, wrapped it up, and tied the rope back around it. I haven't opened it since."

"Oh, David. It's OK. I'll organize Luke's papers, copy what I want, and leave you the originals."

I knew then that I'd place Mom's diary at the bottom of the box.

Sitting on the porch and going through the box, I find copies of Luke's Mississippi diary, but it's just a portion of it, only two out of four sections. *Where are the rest?*

Rutland and Plainfield, Vermont

I've contacted Gail Falk through the Civil Rights Movement Archive website. She's agreed to meet me in Rutland at a café halfway between our homes.

As I am ascending into the Green Mountains, a river beside the road rushes past gray boulders. My breath catches and my heart leaps. *Am I brave enough to do this? Why are my feelings so raw?*

I realize I need to stay present, but long forgotten memories are flooding my mind. *Yes! I can do this. Pay attention to the road. Steady, girl . . .*

We sit outside the café as trucks and cars rumble past. We talk for hours, and I recognize the courageous young woman Luke brought home to Rhode Island in the late summer of 1964.

Gail explains that she has been meeting with other civil rights veterans. "We're planning to hold a reunion called Mississippi Freedom Summer at Fifty. Do you want to go?"

"Yes!" I reply enthusiastically.

During the reunion, Gail and I share a room at a gracious bed and breakfast in downtown Meridian. She takes me under her wing and introduces me to the world and people Luke knew.

A year later, Gail invites me to stay with her and her husband at their home in Vermont. She lugs out cardboard boxes stuffed with files containing her Mississippi letters, newspaper articles, and other paraphernalia.

"Copy whatever you want," she says.

Much time elapses, and my manuscript is nearly finished.
I call her. "Will you be one of my first readers?"
Gail offers invaluable details and insights.

Meridian, Mississippi

It is my first day at the Mississippi reunion. Gail plunges into the
crowd gathered around Mark Levy's photo exhibit at the historic
Temple Theater. She looks for Gwen (Thompson) Chamberlain.
As soon as Gail tells her that I am Luke's little sister, Gwen gently
folds me in her arms.

"Oh Luke!" she exclaims with a wide grin. "I have a picture
back home of Luke riding me around on his back like a horse."

She smiles, and I smile too. I remember how it felt when Luke
galloped around with me on his back when I was a child.

"I was too young for Freedom School, but my older sisters,
Andreesa and Rose—they were in Luke's classes. They *loved* Luke!
Dorothy did too. My sisters couldn't stop talking about him. It was
'Luke this' and 'Luke that.' My sisters are coming. They're driving
down here. You'll get to meet them. I live in San Diego. I'm a jour-
nalist and writer. My sisters Andreesa and Dorothy live in Albany."

Did I hear that right?

"Albany, New York?" I ask.

It had never occurred to me that one day, in Meridian, I might
meet some of Luke's former Freedom School students and—ser-
endipity—that these two sisters would live close to where I do.

In the afternoon, Gail takes us on a short walk to see another
photo exhibit at the art museum. Some of Gail's photos are on
display.

Gwen calls to me from across the room. "Look at this photo!"

As I come closer, she points excitedly. "I told you so. See! My
sisters always wanted to be right there with Luke."

I stare at the photo, amazed.

This same image hung in the middle of the jumble of photos Mom tacked to the wall in her bedroom. Most of the snapshots she chose featured Luke. Over the years, I'd gazed at this photo maybe a million times. Luke is standing in front of the new COFO office surrounded by his young Mississippi friends. Now I learn it is Lance on one arm, Dorothy on the other. Andreesa looks over his shoulder and her sister Rose too. I get goosebumps.

Later in the week, I meet Dorothy Singletary, Andreesa Coleman, and other members of the Thompson sisters' clan at a neighborhood soul-food restaurant. During my stay, Ed Tureaud, the precocious physicist, tells me about his memories of studying biology with Luke and about his work and family life. He proudly discusses his daughter's achievement of being educated as a practical nurse.

Jackson, Mississippi

It is mid-week during the Mississippi reunion in 2014. Each project site is hosting its own events, but this day, everyone from around the state gathers to attend keynote speeches, panels, and workshops at Tougaloo College in the state capital of Jackson. Walking across campus in the afternoon, on my way to a workshop on the environment and climate justice, a man strikes up a conversation. Before we part, he hands me his card: Paul Murray, professor of sociology, Siena College. Paul and his friend, singer/songwriter Reggie Harris, have been traveling with a busload of students from Albany High School, making a civil rights tour of the South. What a coincidence! In Albany, New York—friendship awaits.

Siena College, Loudonville, New York

Back at home, perusing old family photos and letters, I pick up a yellowed envelope. The script is familiar—Luke's handwriting.

Inside is a folded napkin I vaguely remember. I scan the letter and email a copy to Paul, who asks if he can make copies of it for his civil rights class.

Paul has invited Andreesa, Dorothy, and me to visit his class one evening and join a panel to discuss Freedom Summer. In addition to the college students, many visitors, old and young, are jammed close together in the small room. Some students from Albany High School are attending his course too.

Before class begins, Paul tells the students to look carefully at the paper he is handing out. It is a copy of Luke's letter written on a napkin.

"I'm going to ask you, high school students, to show this to your social studies teacher. Explain that this is a *primary document.* What you're holding in your hands is precious." He pauses a moment for emphasis. "It's what historians long to find."

Paul turns toward our panel. "Julie," he begins, "tell us about your brother, Luke."

"I'm told he was cute," I say, turning to Andreesa.

She chuckles and takes off. The students laugh too as the conversation see-saws between the sisters, who are eager to share their vivid memories.

Later, Paul and I agree to trade our writing back and forth for feedback. Paul was a Head Start teacher in Mississippi in 1966 and is writing a memoir for his grandchildren. He agrees without hesitation to be my main reader. Paul keeps reminding me, "Don't let you or your family disappear from the story. What was happening in your lives that related to Luke's? And what role did Judaism play in your family?"

Coming from such a secular background with an atheist father, I have never thought about this question. Then, in my mind's eye, Bubbe's soft eyes appear.

"Luke gave you a great gift in his story. I just want you to do the best job with it you can."

North Chatham, New York (Homebase)

Keeping my teenage grandchildren in mind, I know I need to tell them about American history, as well as family history. They are growing up in the Netherlands and know so little. But when I sit down to continue writing in 2016—the morning after Donald Trump was elected, a voice inside is nudging: *Can't you see? This is a bigger story. It's not just for the grandchildren.*

But if this is a bigger story than one for family, then I'll have to tear it apart and start over.

I have joined a small memoir-writing group up the street at the North Chatham Free Library. At our next meeting, I read a few new passages aloud.

"Julie," Nicole Corey says gently. "You've got to say more about Luke if you want to write for a larger audience."

Judy Green-Berg adds, "Think about Luke now, not just as your brother—someone you know. *We* need to see and hear him. Remember, people reading this won't know him at all."

Little by little, I chip away at the memoir. The writing process is like carving and polishing stone. Finally, I begin to understand that each one of us in the story needs to be fleshed out as a character. *Oh yeah*, I think, *how funny . . . The reader wants to know me too.*

One day over lunch at a local food co-op, my close friend Brin Quell reads from her notes about the manuscript.

"This is a love letter to your brother, but there are silent spaces that want for words. Tell us more about some of the dark family experiences . . . warts and all. Luke was protective, your mother largely absent, your father too. Bubbe was your family's safety zone. I know this is where writing memoir gets tricky."

Gloucester, Massachusetts

Gathering material, I reach out to other veterans of the civil rights movement, including Luke's friend and fellow volunteer Judy Wright. It turns out she is working on a memoir about her experiences of being a Freedom Rider and a volunteer in Meridian. Her husband, Frank, now goes by his nickname, Sib. Although the three of us have never met, they invite me to stay with them.

Getting close to their home, the tiny road narrows as the spit of land juts out into the Atlantic Ocean. Judy greets me warmly, shows me the guest room, and hands me a chapter she has just written about Luke. The next morning, their son Luke, who is named after my brother, joins us for breakfast. Watching over us is the Mexican candelabra my mother gave them as a gift when he was born. Like Gail and many other friends, Judy and Sib didn't realize how swiftly Luke's illness would progress and thus never had the chance to say goodbye.

Kansas City, Missouri

The journey of discovery leads me to Syrtiller Kabat, Luke's wife, as I've always known it would.

"Come visit. Stay with me for as long as you want." On the phone, she explains, "I have a chest full of Luke's things. I don't want to part with them, but I don't have the courage to look at them myself. Warning: there's a lot."

So here I am, in Syrtiller's home office, kneeling beside the large green wooden chest filled with Luke's papers, scrapbooks, and mementos of all kinds. A large manila envelope catches my eye. "For Syrtiller" is written on the outside. I recognize my mother's handwriting. When I open it, many letters tumble out, still in their envelopes, postmark dates visible, each one numbered in sequence by Mom. I carefully arrange them in order on the floor and begin to read these multipage letters, densely handwritten on tiny sheets of notebook paper, scribbled front and back. Soon I realize, *I'll never have time to actually read all these letters! Better to just copy them here and read them when I have time back home.*

Returning from work, Syrtiller tells me that the manila package was a wedding gift my mother gave to her. During the Summer Project, Luke wrote letters almost daily and sent them to his friend Art Zelman at Stanford. Art passed them on to a secretary, who transcribed sections to be published in Stanford's literary magazine, *Sequoia*. When Luke returned from Mississippi at the end of the fall, the secretary bundled up all the letters and sent them, in this very envelope, to our mother who numbered each one. Mom carried this precious envelope with her on the plane when she flew out for their wedding.

Syrtiller admits that she has never opened them. Luke had died so suddenly. It was too much to bear.

So, with trembling hands, I open each letter to the light of day for the first time in over fifty years. Luke had once touched and held these sheets of paper. I hurriedly copy everything, these precious primary documents. There is much more in the chest too, including the *two missing sections* of Luke's diary, plus essays and papers he'd written, letters he'd received, photos he'd taken, and his scrapbooks filled with his handwritten notes. Finally, I have what I need to fill in the gaps and tell much of the story that I am writing *in his own words*.

Besides the chest, there are Syrtiller's stories and the chance for the two of us to reconnect after many years. I learn about the life she lived in the intervening years. I meet her son, Luke Kabat, named after my brother, and two of her grandchildren, Derek Rowe Kabat and Kourtney Haley Kabat. Syrtiller tells me about her third grandchild, Bo San Kwon Beauwin.

In Appreciation
(For Those Not Mentioned in "the Story" Above)

With the passing of time, more grandchildren arrive. Each one is an inspiration adding to the mix—in the Netherlands, younger brother Ben; in Hawaii, twins, Bianca and Luca, my older daughter Tanya D'Avanzo's children.

To all my grandchildren, I say: thank you, each of you, for your eagerness to know your Bubby, the world I came from, and your family roots. To my beautiful daughters, Tanya and Rivke, thank you for the unbounded love you've brought into my life from the moments you were born. And to Wayne, my partner of many years, it's a cliché but true that without you this journey would not have been possible.

To my sister, Alix Van Zant: despite the centrifugal forces Mom encouraged in our early years, as adults, we agreed to work on our relationship and learn how to communicate with each other. The constructive work we've done has nurtured my ability to write about Luke.

My appreciation also goes to my niece Maya, cousins Paul and Karen Shain, friends Susan Griss, Gwen Schwarz, Carl Berg, Don Walker, Pat McGeown, Kim Grethen, David Johns, Kathleen Turley, Karen Halverson, Elissa Kane, and others too numerous to name individually (I trust you know who you are).

To my childhood friends in Rhode Island, Judy Atkins and Allison Allfrey: your friendships shaped my life for the better in more ways than you can know.

To all the children and teens Luke knew in Meridian during Freedom Summer: you've been so generous sharing your memories and reflections. Thanks goes to not only those I've had the pleasure to meet but also those I know from Luke's writings or from your Freedom School essays, which he treasured.

To Freeman Cocroft (deceased): I wish we had had the chance to meet in person. I am grateful to have learned through others of your love for the children, your friendship with Luke, and your deep commitment to the cause of racial justice.

To photographers who were particularly helpful: I was lucky to correspond with Matt Herron before his sudden death. Thank you to fellow volunteers, Mark Levy and Patti Miller, and to Lincoln Cushing, archivist and historian for the Kaiser Permanente Heritage Foundation.

To Paul Rapp, copyright lawyer: what a maze for the novice learning about permissions and citations—you made it so much easier for me to find my way.

To Catherine Parnell, editor in chief of *Consequence Magazine*, focusing on the culture and consequences of war: thank you for pointing out gaps in the story and urging me to drop any efforts to be polite, walk on eggshells, or otherwise avoid ruffling feathers. Writing memoir requires digging in the dirt.

To Tracy Crow: I could not have hoped for a more caring, perceptive, or steadfast literary agent. I will never forget the sound of your laughter when you called to share the good news!

To Emily Snyder Bandy, acquisitions editor, and your dedicated team at the University Press of Mississippi: thank you for appreciating the promise of this book and bringing it to fruition.

✦ ✦ ✦

To Lucien, my brother, I love you. Need I say more? Because of this project, I feel you present in my life again, and it is a blessing.

RESOURCES

Unpublished Writings

Letters and diaries are at the heart of this memoir. Foremost are those written by my brother Luke, who was always scribbling notes. Other unpublished writings were found among Luke's private papers, including letters and speeches he transcribed by hand by Freeman Cocroft, Polly Heidelberg, and Reverend C. T. Vivian, among others. Gail Falk and Judy Wright shared many of their personal letters. Luke collected essays written by the Meridian Freedom School students. He also wrote essays of his own, such as the one about American violence in Vietnam. Sarah Kabat, our mother, kept a diary during the last month of Luke's life. Among her private papers were letters sent after his untimely death—a copy of one sent to Syrtiller by Dr. Robert Glaser, dean of Stanford Medical School, and another by Luke's close friend Irv Weissman, written years afterward.

The only change I made in quoting Luke's handwritten notes was an editorial decision. For the sake of readability, I have replaced most of Luke's idiosyncratic dashes with periods and commas.

Conversations

Conversations with others about their first-hand memories were a major resource, cited wherever they have appeared in the text. I recorded a few of the conversations, which helped me recapture the individual voice of each speaker. I am indebted to the Thompson sisters Andreesa Coleman and Dorothy Singletary, to Gail Falk, Syrtiller Kabat, Ed Tureaud, Lenray Gandy, and Judy Wright.

Photos in Private Collections

Syrtiller has kept Luke's precious scrapbook, filled with snapshots and his handwritten captions. Gail Falk and Judy Wright generously shared their photo collections. Photographer Bill Rodd (deceased), a friend of Gail's, visited Meridian in the fall of 1964. Many of his portraits are in her collection. I scoured old family albums and boxes of scattered snapshots, where I found photos by our father and cousin Paul Shain, a fine photographer who was a professional cameraman on documentary films.

Bibliography

Belfrage, Sally. *Freedom Summer*. New York: Viking Press, 1965.

Bigart, Homer. "Mississippi Test Leads to Arrests: 8 Negro Children Seized after Restaurant Visit." *New York Times*, December 4, 1964, 20. https://www.nytimes .com/1964/12/04/archives/mississippi-test-leads-to-arrests-8-negro-children -seized-after.html.

Bigart, Homer. "Wide Klan Plot Is Hinted in One of 3 Rights Killings." *New York Times*, November 29, 1964, 1, 41. https://www.nytimes.com/1964/11/29/archives/ wide-klan-plot-is-hinted-in-one-of-3-rights-killings.html.

Buckley, Thomas. "CORE Says FBI Has 'Witnesses': Group Helped Mississippi Inquiry, Farmer Asserts." *New York Times*, December 6, 1964, 44.

Carlson, Walter. "Rights Leaders Hail the Arrests but Voice Doubt on Convictions." *New York Times*, December 5, 1964, 18.

Civil Rights Movement Archive. Duke University Libraries, Durham, NC. n.d. Accessed December 22, 2022. https://www.crmvet.org/.

Clark, Willie Joe. Affidavit. November 25, 1964. State of Mississippi, County of Lauderdale.

Cocroft, Mason Freeman. Letter asking permission to return to Mississippi. n.d. Congress of Racial Equality, Mississippi Fourth Congressional District Records, 1961–66. Wisconsin Historical Society, Freedom Summer Digital Collection, 2013. https://content.wisconsinhistory.org/digital/collection/ p15932coll2/id/41869.

CORE. "Personnel Report [Mason Freeman Cocroft]." Civil Rights Movement Archive, n.d. Accessed January 25, 2023. https://www.crmvet.org/docs/640000 _core_cocroft2.pdf.

De Kruif, Paul. *Life among the Doctors*. New York: Harcourt, Brace, and Company, 1949.

Devlin, John C. "Families of Victims Voice Mixed Views on Arrests by FBI." *New York Times*, December 5, 1964, 19.

Dittmer, John. *Local People: The Struggle for Civil Rights in Mississippi*. Champaign: University of Illinois Press, 1994.

Doar, John. Memorandum to director of the Federal Bureau of Investigation concerning harassment of Gail Falk by Meridian Police on Thanksgiving Day, 1964, Department of Justice, February 5, 1965.

Falk, Gail. "Being Jewish in Meridian—Part 1." Freedom Songs, December 30, 2011. https://freedomsongs11.wordpress.com/2011/12/.

Falk, Gail. "Freedom Songs." Freedom Songs, February 5, 2012. https://freedom songs11.wordpress.com/2012/02/05/freedom-songs/.

Falk, Gail. "Pittsburgh Girl Pens Shocking Story about Mississippi Jails," *Pittsburgh Courier*. January 4, 1965, n.p. News clipping, Gail Falk's private papers.

Falk, Gail. "Remembering Freedom Summer." Address to state-wide conference of Mississippi Young Professionals, Meridian, Mississippi, 2013. Civil Rights Movement Archive, n.d. Accessed January 25, 2023. https://www.crmvet.org/nars/falk64.htm.

Feron, James. "Dr. King Accepts Nobel Peace Prize as 'Trustee.'" *New York Times*, December 11, 1964, 1, 32.

Feron, James. "Dr. King Stresses Nonviolence Role: Oslo Students Nations Should Try to 'Sacrifice' to Achieve World Peace." *New York Times*, December 12, 1964, 1, 18.

Freedom School. "A Prospectus for the Summer." Letter sent to prospective volunteers, spring 1964, Luke Kabat's private papers. Available online as "Prospectus for the Mississippi Freedom Summer," Civil Rights Movement Archive, n.d. Accessed January 25, 2023. https://www.crmvet.org/docs/fs64_proposal.pdf.

Goodman, Carolyn, with Brad Herzog. *My Mantelpiece: A Memoir of Survival and Social Justice*. Pacific Grove: Why Not Books, 2014.

Hampton, Henry, dir. *Eyes on the Prize*. Season 1, episode 1, "Awakening." Aired January 21, 1987, on PBS.

Herbers, John. "At Chaney Memorial Service." *New York Times*, August 8, 1964, 7.

Herbers, John. "Dam Is Situated in Desolate Area." *New York Times*, August 6, 1964, 16.

Herbers, John. "FBI Arrests 21 in Mississippi in Murder of 3 Rights Workers; Law Officers and Pastor Held." *New York Times*, December 5, 1964, 1, 18.

Herbers, John. "Mississippians Raise Funds for 21 Held in Killings." *New York Times*, December 7, 1964, 38.

Herbers, John. "Mississippi Bars Rights Trial Now: Declines to Take Immediate Action against 21 Seized in Philadelphia Slayings." *New York Times*, December 6, 1964, 1, 43.

Herbers, John. "Neshoba County Fair Unclouded by Murder of Rights Workers." *New York Times*, August 9, 1964, 62.

Herbers, John. "Speakers Pour Out Bitterness at Chaney Memorial Service." *New York Times*, August 8, 1964, 7.

Herbers, John. "US Aide Frees 19 in Rights Deaths; Bars FBI's Data: Commissioner at a Hearing Rejects Testimony about a Signed Confession." *New York Times*, December 11, 1964, 1, 34.

Herron, Matt. *Mississippi Eyes: The Story of Photography of the Southern Documentary Project*. San Rafael: Talking Fingers Publications, 2014.

Hughes, Langston. *The Collected Works of Langston Hughes*. Edited by Arnold Rampersad. New York: Penguin Random House, 1994.

Izadi, Elahe. "Why Hundreds of American Newsrooms Have Started Capitalizing the 'b' in 'Black.'" Washington Post, June 18, 2020. https://www.washingtonpost.com/lifestyle/media/

why-hundreds-of-american-newsrooms-have-started-capitalizing-the-b-in
-black/2020/06/18/7687a7a8-b16e-11ea-8f56-63f38c990077_story.html.

Kabat, Luke. "Letters by Luke Kabat." *Sequoia: Stanford Literary Magazine* 2 (winter 1965), 14–24.

Kabat, Luke. "My Friends in Mississippi." *New Republic*, May 29, 1965, 18–20.

Kabat, Luke. "Notes from the County Jail." *Stanford Challenger*, February 1965, 29–40.

Kabat, Luke. "The Violent American." Unpublished manuscript, spring 1965, author's private papers.

Kenworthy, E. W. "Resolution Wins." *New York Times*, August 8, 1964, 1–2.

Knap, Ted. "A Rights Volunteer Speaks for All . . . 'Felt I Was Needed.' An Interview with Gail Falk." *New York World Telegram and Sun*, June 30, 1964, n.p. News clipping, Gail Falk's private papers.

Lewis, David Levering. *Du Bois, W. E. B., 1919–1963: The Fight for Equality and the American Century*. New York: Henry Holt and Company, 2000.

Lewis, John. *Walking with the Wind: A Memoir of the Movement*. New York: Harcourt Brace & Company, 1998.

Lynd, Staughton. "The Freedom Schools: Concept And Organization." History Is a Weapon, n.d. Accessed January 25, 2023. https://www.historyisaweapon.com/defcon1/lynfresch.html/.

Mark Levy Collection. Queens College/CUNY Rosenthal Library Archives, Queens, NY. n.d. Accessed December 22, 2022. https://archives.qc.cuny.edu/civilrights/collections/show/1.

Martínez, Elizabeth Sutherland, ed. *Letters from Mississippi*. Brookline: Zephyr Press, 2002.

Minear, Lawrence. "Freedom School in Miss.: RI Man Teaches Biology Class." *Providence Sunday Journal*, August 23, 1964, N-28.

New York Times. "Arrests by FBI Praised in South: Major Papers Laud Work in Mississippi Rights Deaths." December 7, 1964, 39.

New York Times. "FBI and Sailors Joined Wide Hunt; 6-Week Search for 3 Men Went on without Let-Up," August 5, 1964, 37.

New York Times. "FBI Declines Comment." December 6, 1964, 44.

New York Times. "FBI Finds 3 Bodies Believed to Be Rights Workers." August 5, 1964, 1. https://www.nytimes.com/1964/12/07/archives/arrests-by-fbi-praised -in-south-major-papers-laud-work-in.html.

New York Times. "Special to the *New York Times*: President Vows Quick Results in Mississippi Slaying Inquiry." August 9, 1964, 1, 48.

New York Times. "Went into State to Enroll Voters: Burning of a Negro Church in Neshoba County Drew Them to Their Doom." December 5, 1964, 19.

Niebuhr, Rheinhold. *Mississippi Black Paper: Fifty-Seven Negro and White Citizens' Testimony of Police Brutality, the Breakdown of Law and Order and the Corruption of Justice in Mississippi*. New York: Random House, 1965.

Popkin, George. "'I Knew Death Was a Real Thing': A Rights Worker Tells Why." *Providence Evening Bulletin*, n.d., 1, 3. News clipping, author's private papers.

Sandel, M. Elizabeth. "Dr. Herman Kabat: Neuroscience in Translation . . . From Bench to Bedside." *American Academy of Physical Medicine and Rehabilitation* 5 (June 2013). https://onlinelibrary.wiley.com/doi/pdf/10.1016/j.pmrj.2013.04.020.

Schwerner, Rita L. "Testimony of Rita L. Schwerner." History Is a Weapon, n.d. Accessed January 25, 2023. https://www.historyisaweapon.com/defcon1/schwernertestimony.html.

Sims, Bernice. *Detour before Midnight: Freedom Summer Workers James Chaney, Michael Schwerner and Andrew Goodman Made an Unscheduled Stop.* Mineola: SimsBernice713, 2014.

Sitton, Claude. "Chaney Was Given a Brutal Beating; Re-examination Is Made of Slain Rights Worker." *New York Times*, August 8, 1964, 7.

Sitton, Claude. "Graves at a Dam; Discovery Is Made in New Earth Mound in Mississippi. *New York Times*, August 5, 1964, 1.

Spain, David. "Mississippi Autopsy (Ramparts Magazine's Mississippi Eyewitness [1964], pp. 43–49)." Dick Atlee, last modified April 28, 2019. http://dickatlee.com/issues/mississippi/mississippi_eyewitness/pdfs/mississippi_autopsy.pdf.

Stanford University. "1960s." Student Life: Decade by Decade, Stanford Stories from the Archive, n.d. Accessed January 25, 2023. https://exhibits.stanford.edu/stanford-stories/feature/1960s.

Wright, Judith Frieze. *Acts of Resistance: A Freedom Rider Looks Back on the Civil Rights Movement.* n.p.: Apple Bay, 2019.

INDEX

ABOUT THE AUTHOR

Photo by Tanya D'Avanzo

After graduating magna cum laude from Brandeis University with a BA in philosophy, Julie Kabat returned to her heart's calling of music and embarked on a twenty-year career as an avant-garde composer/performer, singer, and storyteller, touring the United States, Canada, and Japan. She also devoted herself to teaching and was recognized as a pioneer in the field of arts in education. For over forty years, she worked as a teaching artist in inner city and rural schools, empowering young people to discover an authentic writer's voice while learning how to write poems, stories, and plays that they set to music and performed. Along the way, Julie raised her two daughters as a single mom and now visits her five grandchildren who live in Hawaii and the Netherlands. She resides with her life partner, Wayne Shelton, and their cat in the beautiful Hudson River Valley down the street from the North Chatham Free Library where she is a longtime trustee. She enjoys taking long walks on country roads, practicing piano, and singing to the birds, hoping that they too take pleasure in dialogue.